"With prices soaring higher than i[...] everywhere need to learn what C[...] *Your Dollars*. She knows her stuff [...] by cutting the cost of just about e[...]
—Mary Hunt, aut[...]
and *Raising Financially Confident Kids*

"Carrie Rocha has hit a home run with *Pocket Your Dollars*. Not only does she provide a fresh approach to the topic of finances, but she also gives practical advice on how to follow through. Carrie's words carry great weight because she's 'been there, done that' when it comes to digging out of consumer debt. Whether she's giving advice on stretching a dollar or tracking it, she's right on the money with her timely and sound advice. This is a book for every family who wants to live in financial freedom and have a future that is debt free."
—Ellie Kay, America's Family Financial Expert®
and bestselling author of *Living Rich for Less*

"This book is a blueprint to financial prosperity. Smart money management is more about mind-set than it is about math, and Rocha shows readers how to change their attitudes toward saving and spending. It's highly motivating for those ready to choose change."
—J. D. Roth, founder of GetRichSlowly.org
and author of *Your Money: The Missing Manual*

"Carrie's blog has saved me money. This book will transform your relationship with money for the better . . . and for life."
—Tory Johnson, founder of Spark and Hustle
and *New York Times* bestselling author

"I highly recommend *Pocket Your Dollars*. It's perfect for those who want to fix their finances but don't want another budgeting or money management system. This book addresses the root causes behind most money problems."
—Will Chen, co-founder of Wisebread.com

"While for many people money is a source of stress and shame, Carrie knows that it is just a tool. In this smart little book, she shows you how to change your money attitudes so you can pocket more dollars and still build the life you want."

—Laura Vanderkam, author of *All the Money in the World* and *168 Hours*

"This is a must-read for anyone who doesn't know why they can't make their budget work. Carrie will help you figure out what makes you tick when it comes to money. I highly recommend this book."

—Stephanie Nelson, The Coupon Mom, www.couponmom.com

"*Pocket Your Dollars* is much more than a personal finance book. It's a wake-up call that shows you how you put your money where your true values are. Engaging and inspiring, it can give you hope, no matter where you are financially."

—Gerri Detweiler, national credit expert and host of *Talk Credit Radio*

"*Pocket Your Dollars* is the most simple and straightforward book on personal finance that I have ever read. Carrie Rocha frankly shares her own financial failures and successes in a way that will encourage you that financial success is possible—and shockingly, it has very little to do with how much money you make."

—Robin O'Bryant, bestselling author of *Ketchup Is a Vegetable and Other Lies Moms Tell Themselves*

"Anyone who has laid awake in bed thinking about money should read *Pocket Your Dollars*. From her experience, Carrie knows the type of thinking that can get you trapped in a cycle of money worry. She'll show you how to get out."

—Sandra Hanna, CEO of Smartcookies.com and popular media personality

"The practical part of personal finance is easy: Spend less than you earn. In *Pocket Your Dollars*, Carrie uses her wisdom and experience to guide you through the more difficult process of changing your mind-set to be able to consistently build and preserve wealth. Get ready to change your attitude about money."

—Philip Taylor, founder of the national Financial Bloggers Conference and creator of the popular blog PTMoney.com

pocket YOUR DOLLARS

— 5 —
attitude changes
that will help you pay down debt,
avoid financial stress, &
keep more of what you make

CARRIE ROCHA

BETHANY HOUSE PUBLISHERS
a division of Baker Publishing Group
Minneapolis, Minnesota

Published by Bethany House Publishers
11400 Hampshire Avenue South
Bloomington, Minnesota 55438
www.bethanyhouse.com

Bethany House Publishers is a division of
Baker Publishing Group, Grand Rapids, Michigan

Printed in the United States of America

ISBN 978-0-7642-1087-7 (pbk.)

Library of Congress Cataloging-in-Publication Data is available for this title.

Scripture quotations are from the Good News Translation—Second Edition. Copyright
© 1992 by American Bible Society. Used by permission.

The internet addresses, email addresses, and phone numbers in this book are accurate
at the time of publication. They are provided as a resource. Baker Publishing Group
does not endorse them or vouch for their content or permanence.

Cover design by Brand Navigation

13   14   15   16   17   18   19   7   6   5   4   3   2   1

To Marco,
whose internal compass
has never led us astray.

contents

SECTION THREE
now that you're ready,
some simple budgeting advice

1

my story

I grew up in a home where I never lacked. If I wanted something, I eventually got it. I wasn't spoiled and demanding; it was more like I expressed interest in a new toy, new clothes, or a new food I saw on TV, and my parents would take notice. At my next birthday or a special occasion, I'd find that item sitting on the table, wrapped up with a big bow. My mom allowed us to try most new foods that hit the market, no matter how expensive or un-kid-friendly they seemed. I was taken back-to-school clothes shopping every August and given a chance to pick out a set number of brand-new outfits.

My parents met all my basic needs and more during those years. As a result, I never thought about money. Well, I thought about how to *spend* it. On Fridays my brother and I would get an allowance, then ride our bikes to a nearby gas station. We'd spend every penny, to the penny, on candy, then ride home with our pockets full of treasures.

One time my parents tried to introduce us to the concept of savings. For Christmas they gave me a passbook for a savings account. "What is this?" I asked. My dad explained that it was a savings account with fifty dollars in it.

I couldn't understand the purpose. I found myself wondering, *Why would I leave fifty dollars in the bank with my name on it when I could take it out and spend it?* I don't remember how my parents attempted to explain it to me, but I never saw it their way. In a matter of time, they acquiesced and hauled my brother and me to the bank, where we withdrew our money and closed those seemingly useless savings accounts.

My carefree, fun, and prosperous childhood years ended abruptly in August of 1985. For as long as I could remember, my parents owned a secondhand consignment store. It was like a giant thrift store with everything from clothes to furniture, electronics, housewares, books, and antiques, all sold on consignment. When the lease for the space was up that summer, the landlord didn't renew it. He had other more lucrative plans for the building.

I remember the scramble my parents had to try to find a new location. We wanted the same neighborhood, but it had to be zoned properly to allow a retail storefront. They couldn't find one in time, so they sold all the inventory and closed the doors for good.

That store was our family's mainstay, and we all felt scared when we lost it. Sure, my mom worked outside the home in an office job, but it didn't earn anything close to what the store had provided. To make ends meet, my dad picked up a graveyard shift as a gas station clerk while he interviewed for full-time positions by day.

That was nearly thirty years ago, but I remember it clearly because that's when I began to worry about money. It started with a recurring dream about lack. I dreamed that my family didn't have enough money to buy my school supplies. I arrived to the first day of fifth grade with the same pencil box I used in fourth grade, becoming the school's laughingstock. I was afraid of what my friends would think of me now that my family didn't have the money we once did.

As a nine-year-old girl, I worried about money in other ways too. I wondered whether my parents would have enough to buy my school lunch. At Christmas I feared not getting any gifts. I wondered whether I'd get new clothes when I outgrew the ones I had. Our financial future felt uncertain, and I felt powerless to change it.

My fears about money grew worse when my parents divorced in 1988. Our already-tight finances became even tighter. I often had "No, honey, we can't afford it" conversations with my parents when I asked to do or have the things I saw my friends enjoying. I often felt like a financial burden to my parents, even though we tried to use our creativity to acquire most of the things I desired.

I entered adulthood afraid of money. Success seemed even scarier than lack, perhaps because I saw my parents' success fade almost overnight. I lived through the stress that this created in our family, and eventually I saw it divide my family by divorce.

I found lack to be a more comfortable emotional place. I couldn't imagine a scenario where I'd be able to provide for myself. I figured if my parents struggled to provide for me, then there was no way I could do any better on my own.

Marco's Brazilian Start

My husband, Marco, grew up in a very different world from my suburban Minneapolis upbringing. He was raised in Rio de Janeiro, Brazil. All five of his family members lived in a

11

two-bedroom condo his parents owned outright. Space was obviously tight. His parents slept in one room, his sister got the other bedroom, and Marco and his brother shared the living room. By Brazilian standards they were an average, middle-class family.

Marco sometimes asked for elaborate toys or fancy things, but he always knew what his mom would say: "No, honey, it's too expensive and we can't afford it." One time he played with an electric race car set at a friend's house and begged his mom to buy one. He didn't get it, but even today he thinks of it and wants to buy one for our girls.

His family did occasionally splurge. In Marco's house, a splurge was something as simple—by American standards— as a pint of ice cream. No more than once a year did they enjoy such a tremendous treat.

Marco's dad had a military pension and owned a small moving company. They had a decent income, but inflation eroded much of it. Through the 1970s and 1980s, Brazilian inflation averaged 100 percent, which means the cost of goods doubled each year. At one point it reached 1,000 percent, which made a $10 item cost $110 a year later.[1]

With astronomical inflation came sky-high interest rates. You didn't take debt lightly because your interest rate changed each month, increasing as inflation went up. When Marco's dad bought two additional condos to keep as rental proper-ties, he financed them, but not with a thirty-year mortgage like Americans do. He put 60 to 70 percent down, then paid the remainder to the previous owner within eighteen months.

Marco learned that in Brazil you can't have everything you want. No one he knew did. Yet it seemed like Americans, at least the ones he saw on TV, got everything they wished for. Hollywood portrayed typical American life as one with huge houses, sprawling yards, shiny cars, and kids with a ton of toys and freedom from lack. He always wanted to go to the United States so he could enjoy that same abundance he saw portrayed on TV.

Marco entered adulthood eager to have the things money can buy. In his mind, success was marked by what you possessed and how much money you made. He never wanted to hear "No, we can't afford it" again.

Almost $60,000 in Debt

When Marco and I got married, I bragged to friends, family, and the pastor—anyone who would listen, really—that we had pulled off a debt-free wedding. But I was being a hypocrite. Yes, it's true that our wedding ceremony and reception were paid for in cash, but what I neglected to tell anyone was that both my ring and our honeymoon were funded, in their entirety, with credit cards.

Something inside me longed for a debt-free life, but that was not the life we lived. By the time we had been married for two and a half years, we had nearly $60,000 in debt. We both had decent jobs. We didn't see any gaping financial holes. Yet we'd somehow amassed debt nearly equal to one year's wages.

In addition to our mortgage, here's what our debt included:

- **Credit cards.** We had a major credit card and some store-issued cards. We were still paying for my ring, our honeymoon, plus furniture and who-knows-what other consumer goods we'd purchased over the years.
- **A car loan.** We rejoiced the day we found out we were approved for 100 percent financing on that vehicle.

13

- **Family.** We'd both borrowed money from family to cover emergencies at different times and wanted to repay them.
- **Lawyer.** We needed legal counsel on a matter but it didn't fit within our budget, so we put it on a payment plan.
- **Assessment on our townhouse.** Our townhouse association put new siding on our complex, and our portion of the cost was $7,000.
- **Student loans.** Marco had student loans, but he didn't have a college degree to show for it.
- **Tax debt.** Marco was carrying this debt, which resulted from some unwise financial decisions in his past.

We also had a $170,000 mortgage on a two-bedroom townhouse. I bought it a few months before we were married and mortgaged 100 percent of the purchase price.

Our Path Out

We were shocked in the spring of 2006 when we took account and realized the amount of debt we had. For a few weeks after that, we grappled with some very serious questions, like "How did we get here?" and "Where will we end up if we don't stop ourselves?"

I remember a particular conversation Marco and I had, where we calculated how much money we'd cumulatively earned over the previous ten years. It was well over half a million dollars. Then we looked at each other and said, "What do we have to show for half a million dollars?" The answer: $60,000 in debt. How could that be possible?

We were ready to make a change. We wanted our lives to amount to something different than that. We had dreams of living overseas in Brazil and working full time to enrich the lives of Marco's countrymen. We weren't ready to give that up.

In June 2006 we made two decisions that changed our lives.

1. We decided to get out of debt.
2. We decided that we would stay out of debt for the rest of our lives.

And so we did. It took thirty months, which is exactly two and a half years, but in November 2009 I wrote the check that paid off the last of our non-mortgage debts.

To date we have avoided incurring any new debt (other than moving houses recently and replacing our old mortgage with a new mortgage, which I explain in more detail in chapter 5, "I'll Fake It 'Til I Make It"). We've self-funded Marco's graduate degree, a three-year-old minivan, and every other curveball life has thrown at us since June 2006.

Our Attitude Changes

The question I'm always asked when I tell our story about getting out and staying out of debt is "How did you do it?" And my answer is always "We changed our attitudes toward money." An attitude is a disposition, orientation, or mental or emotional outlook on something.[2] As Marco and I changed our outlook about money, we were able to make decisions consistent with our goals. Prior to that, we said we wanted financial success and stability, but our actions didn't line up with what we said.

At the start of our financial journey, our attitudes sounded like this:

- "If only I had more money, then I wouldn't have so many money problems."
- "It has been a rough day. I deserve to treat myself to dinner out tonight."
- "We don't have to save money for our car's next brake job. We'll cross that bridge when we come to it."
- "If it's on sale, then I have permission to buy it."
- "Wealth is demonstrated by what you own."

Seven years and no new debt later, we sound more like this:

- "Financial success isn't about how much you make, but about what you do with what you make."
- "I work too hard for my money to spend it on fruitless things."
- "It's our responsibility today to plan for tomorrow's expenses."
- "Most of America's wealthy aren't showing it off."

Behavior Change Is What We Really Want

Although this is a book about attitude changes, we all ultimately want to make behavioral changes. To bring about change in your finances, you need to save, spend, and/or account for your money in a different way than you are doing today. There is no question about that. However, my approach to the changes required of you is not centered on changing each individual problematic behavior. Life is too varied and too complex for us to make meaningful changes one problematic behavior at a time.

Let's say you want to lose twenty-five pounds. You decide that the one thing you need to do is get back into running.

Effective immediately, you'll lace up your sneakers after dinner and head out for a vigorous run. That beats plopping down on the couch for a few hours of TV and Facebook.

That works okay for a few days, until you eat dinner out one night. You aren't home to lace up your sneakers, so you skip the run. Then it rains for a few days straight and again, you can't head out. Now school's back in session and you need to help your kids with their homework and get them to bed earlier; an evening run doesn't fit into your schedule anymore. Your plan to lose weight is thwarted. Circumstances don't line up exactly as you'd hoped, and you've excused yourself from modifying your behavior.

A better approach would be to start with an honest look at the underlying issues of why you've gained the weight. Maybe it's low self-esteem due to a recent divorce, stress from financial pressure, boredom at work, or a hopelessness that change is possible for you. Once you uncover and deal with the real issue, then eating healthier and living a more active lifestyle are more easily sustained.

Attitudes Are Roots

When Marco and I determined to get out of debt, our first step wasn't a laundry list of no-no behaviors. And yours isn't either. (Yes, I heard that sigh of relief.) After deciding to get out and stay out of debt, the first thing we did was replace the attitude "If only I had more money" with "I can choose my own financial future." It's not about how much money you make; it's about what you do with what you make.

This was an effective first step for us because it was manageable. That means we actually did it without quitting. Additionally, it was intertwined with a handful of other attitudes that we didn't know we had. One at a time, we realized additional unhealthy beliefs, perceptions, and outlooks we had on money, and changed them. Each one was manageable. Each one was powerful. Each one made making right choices a lot easier.

It's like we pulled a dandelion out by the roots rather than simply popping off the flower. When our faulty attitudes were uprooted, behaviors like these couldn't grow back:

- Judging affordability by the monthly payment and not by the overall price
- Routinely bouncing checks
- Paying every bill on the last possible day of the grace period
- Purposely setting up our tax withholdings so we'd get a huge annual refund
- Planning our main recreational activities around spending money—either going to the mall or out to eat
- Spending over $1,000 on Christmas gifts before we even had kids
- Going on spontaneous weekend getaways paid for by credit cards

Acting on Attitudes

Decision making is a complex process. Attitudes play a large role, but they don't work alone. You think about the immediate impact, feel peer pressure, and are influenced by your overall emotional and physical state. At times you feel too tired to do the right thing or fear the social consequence of standing up for what you think. It happens to all of us.

18

Our attitudes can have an increasingly larger voice in both the split-second and belabored choices we make. Three things give you power to act in ways that are consistent with your beliefs.

Awareness

When making a deliberate decision, how can you act on something you aren't even thinking about? When you consider making a large purchase like a home, you stop and think through your attitudes, even though you don't call them "attitudes" in the moment. Your attitudes influence how you answer questions like "How do I feel about having a fixer-upper?" or "Do I prefer a large house with a small yard or a smaller house with a large yard?" Whatever house you buy is a direct result of how you answer these kinds of questions.

Even in a knee-jerk spontaneous decision, your attitudes often spring up like a reflex and influence your split-second choice. I don't care much for spiders, but I don't go through my day consciously thinking about them. A few years ago I was reading a *National Geographic* with a four-page photo spread in the magazine's center. As I opened up the foldout, I saw a photograph of a tarantula. At the sight of the spider's image, I screamed and threw the magazine from my lap to the floor. My attitude against spiders manifested in that moment. When you make spur-of-the-moment decisions about money, your attitudes influence what you decide.

Awareness answers the question "What do I believe?" In this book I share five things Marco and I believed about money. Until we started to get out of debt, I couldn't have articulated those attitudes. They existed, but I wasn't consciously aware of them. This book will jump-start your awareness about

19

your own attitudes toward money. From there you can replace undesirable attitudes and cultivate those you want to grow.

Strength

Strong attitudes exert more influence on behavior than their weaker counterparts. Think about the Founding Fathers of the United States. They believed that government should be something different from what they were experiencing at the time. I'm certain they *really* believed in their cause. I can judge the strength of their beliefs by the boldness of their actions. These men launched a revolution and war against Britain, then worked tirelessly to create a framework for this new country and took responsibility to lead it. Their convictions were so strong that some even gave their lives to defend what they believed.

Especially in knee-jerk situations, where you aren't logically sorting through your beliefs, your strongest attitudes trump. They spring up so loudly and so clearly that they drown out other quieter attitudes. It's important, then, to strengthen the attitudes that you want to drive your behavior.

Direct experience is the best way to strengthen a belief. Pretend that you don't often buy frozen pizza. You prefer homemade pizza. You've seen a million TV commercials touting frozen pizzas with homemade flavor, but none of them sway you. One day at the grocery store you're given a free sample of a new pizza. You enjoy it. In fact, you like it well enough to actually buy a couple of those frozen pizzas. Tasting the pizza (a direct experience) was able to motivate you to act (buy pizza) in ways that watching a TV commercial (indirect experience) was never able to.

Strength answers the question "How much do I believe?" In explaining each attitude, I give you opportunities to take action yourself. These action steps can provide you with first-hand, direct experiences with each new positive attitude as a first step in strengthening them within you.

Motivation

Motivation plays a major role in the staying power of an attitude. There are three primary reasons people embrace certain attitudes: (1) to comply with an authority figure, (2) to fit in with a person or group, or (3) for an internalized, personal reason. If you embrace a perspective because you want to comply or fit in, then your motivation is external. When that external factor disappears, your motivation wanes and your attitude regresses.

People who embrace attitudes for internalized, personal reasons are the most successful in acting consistently with their beliefs. Their actions spring from an intrinsic motivation, which is much more powerful over the long term than external motivations. We see this in smokers who want to quit. Those who were motivated by an intrinsic desire to quit are almost two times as successful as those who are motivated by something external like a monetary reward.[3] Not just that, but the intrinsically motivated former smokers are far less likely to relapse than their reward-oriented counterparts.[4]

Motivation answers the question "Why are you doing this?" Those who will be most successful after reading this book are those who internally and personally want to change. Those who are reading to appease a spouse or because it's their book club's choice this month are less likely to act on the things they learn. But even if you've picked up this book for some external reason, I hope it plants a desire for change that becomes your own driving force.

the five attitudes that must go

*Y*ou can see that Marco and I are pretty regular folks who experienced pretty amazing change. It started with a commitment to change. That's your first step too.

I'll help you, over the next five chapters, figure out what to change and why. We'll talk about five attitudes toward money that are influencing the behaviors you don't like.

From there I'll teach you *how* to actually change an attitude so that it sticks. I'll conclude with a few nuts-and-bolts chapters that give budgeting and money-saving advice.

What you are about to learn will help you. Whether you are penniless or a millionaire, this book is for you. Whether you've tried every financial program out there or are making a first-time commitment to improve your situation, this book is for you.

Attitudes influence us all.

2

if only I had more money

The price of greatness is responsibility.
—Winston Churchill

I was in eighth grade when my parents split up. My dad moved out on December 1, 1988, leaving my mom, my younger brother, and me at home. We had a maroon, mid-'80s Buick Skylark that took the three of us everywhere we needed to go. I have no idea what the monthly payment was for that car, but I knew my mom borrowed money to pay for it.

I also knew that things were much tighter financially after my dad moved out than they were before. When I wanted to go on weekend church retreats with my junior high friends, I always had my mom's permission, but I could go only if the church would give me a scholarship. It was the same thing with an overnight field trip with my science class. My mom

25

wanted me to go, but I had to ask the teacher if I could pay a discounted fee because we couldn't afford the full price.

No wonder I felt such hope when I heard my mom explain, "Carrie, next month is our last car payment. *Then* we will have more money." I waited for the change, just like she did. But nothing changed. A few years later we lost our house to foreclosure and downsized from a four-bedroom, four-level home with a yard that backed up to a park to a two-bedroom apartment with a balcony. I was away at college by then, so I spent the summer months and vacations at my grandma's, since she had space enough for me.

I mean no disrespect to my mom by sharing this story. She is a wonderful and caring woman who desired nothing more than to abundantly provide for her family. It wasn't that she lacked will. It wasn't that she was lying when she told me that things would change. To her core she believed that after our Buick Skylark was paid off, our finances would be better.

I Became My Mom

Why didn't the extra money make a difference? Why did things actually get *worse* when our family had *more* discretionary income? I didn't begin to understand it until years later when money-related conversations between Marco and me sounded like this:

> **Marco:** I need a new winter coat. The lining in my old one is ripped.
>
> **Carrie:** I don't think we can afford it. The car insurance is due this month, plus our heating bill is going to be huge. We can't handle a discretionary expense like that right now.

Marco: How can we make an above-average salary, have no kids, and still not afford a new winter coat? How is that possible? Where is the money going?

Carrie: I have no idea. But look, next month you get paid three times. We'll get on track with that third paycheck. *Then* we'll have more money.

I had become my mom. I waited for three-paycheck months because *then* we could afford things that were otherwise out of reach. I also waited for annual bonuses, pay raises, and tax refunds. I don't think I'm alone. With almost 50 percent of American families living paycheck to paycheck,[1] I'm sure this conversation is more commonplace than just my kitchen table. For much of Middle America, we work hard, earn a livable wage, and don't live extravagantly, but we still don't feel very good about our financial situation. Maybe we are one paycheck away from missing a mortgage payment. Maybe we haven't saved a dime for our kids' education or retirement. Maybe we can't imagine a family vacation to Florida without picturing a mound of credit card debt.

We wait for a windfall. Or a promotion. Or a tax refund. Or Grandma's annual cash gift at Christmas. We wait for more money to arrive on our doorstep, believing that when it does, *then* we can begin to change our financial life. Some of us will wait a lifetime, always hoping the next big financial break lies around the corner.

The Heart of the Matter

Personal responsibility is the core issue. When we believe that our financial problems are caused solely by a lack of money, we refuse to acknowledge our current situation as something we've brought about. We deny the fact that the power for changing our future lies within us. And if we continue to deny this fact, change will never come.

For a plethora of reasons, we believe it isn't our fault. "The chips just haven't fallen in my favor," you tell yourself. It may be true that your ex-husband made poor decisions and now you're stuck dealing with them. Or an unforeseen medical emergency resulted in a pile of debt. Each of us has a backstory about how we made a decent living yet became stuck financially.

Imagine a young boy named Chris, whose father was a violent alcoholic. His mom worked multiple jobs to make ends meet, leaving him to fend for himself most of the time. When she was around, she attempted to shelter Chris from Dad's ferocious temper, but it didn't work. Dad's words still cut deeply into Chris's soul. Unsurprisingly, Chris got mixed up with the wrong kids at school and started dabbling with alcohol and cigarettes at age eleven. By the time he was twenty-two, his rap sheet included two felony burglaries and check forging. As part of a plea bargain, he ended up in treatment.

When his counselor asked "Why are you here?" Chris plunged into a lengthy story about his dad's drunken rages and his mom's neglect as she worked hard to put food on the table. "While all that is true and terribly painful," the counselor told him, "you're here because you chose to drink. Your drinking fueled other bad choices. Your childhood might not have been what you desired, but you have the power to choose your response to it. No one can ever take that away from you."

So it is with us and our money. Life may have dealt us an unfair blow compared to the kid down the street. Your choices to overspend, underinvest, and overborrow might have roots in your past. Your parents may not have modeled financial responsibility. Your former business partner might have cooked the books. Your investment advisor might have pilfered away your savings. You can't change the fact that any of that happened, but you still have the power to control your response. No one can take that away from you.

You are responsible to create the future you want to have.

Step one in taking personal responsibility is facing your past and accepting your current situation. From there you have to take responsibility for your future.

Money is not responsible for creating a different reality in your life. If you want something different, then *you* are responsible to create it with the money you have. Your money is a tool at your disposal with which you can carve the path you want to walk. It's remarkable how much this change in attitude changes everything else. Budgets are good and spreadsheets are helpful, but long-term solutions come from changing your mind-set about money.

It's Not How Much You Make

It seems hard to believe that just a little more wiggle room in the monthly budget wouldn't make some sort of positive impact. It reminds me of Luther Elliss's story. He was a professional football player who made $20 million over ten years in the NFL. That's about $167,000 every month for those ten years. Five years after leaving the league, which is half as long as he played, not one dime of the $20 million remained. Elliss was so destitute at that point that he turned to handouts from churches and friends to sustain his family while working as an insurance salesman, making less than $1,500 per month.[2]

Luther Elliss isn't the only striking example of this truth. Economists studied a group of big winners in Florida's Fantasy 5 lottery. Each won $50,000 to $150,000 via a lottery windfall. The winners' average debt at the time of their big wins was $49,000. You might think that they'd pay off their debt and be set on a new course for their lives. But that didn't happen. The study found that three to five years after winning the lottery, the winners were *just as likely* to file bankruptcy as the general population. The authors concluded, "The results show that giving $50,000 to $150,000 to people only postpones bankruptcy." It doesn't prevent it.[3]

> *It doesn't matter how much money you make. What makes a difference is how much money you keep.*

A Wheel Is Missing

If you've felt like your financial life has not gotten traction, then personal responsibility is the first place to look. As your income has gone up over the years, you may have noticed that your expenses tend to grow and even outpace the increase. You feel more broke the more money you have.

On the other hand, maybe you haven't gotten a raise or bonus in years. Or perhaps your income has even decreased. For you, it's hard to believe more money wouldn't change things, because all you've ever known is scrimping and saving. You're sure, with your thrifty ways, that you're an exception to what I'm talking about.

But still your financial life is missing traction. You're like a girl whose bike is broken. After tinkering with it to no avail, she goes into the house and tells her mom that the bike needs a tune-up. Mom comes into the garage to check it out and says, "Honey, a tune-up won't help because you're missing the front wheel." When a fundamental building block is missing from our lives, then no amount of fine-tuning can move things forward. That's why we're not starting with budget worksheets and expense trackers. Those are mechanisms for fine-tuning once we have a solid foundation.

I'll Quit Eating Donuts

I need to pause and clarify something. While I am saying that more money alone is not enough to resolve your financial issues, I am not naïve enough to suggest that your bank balance or income level doesn't play a role in your financial life. Of course it does. What I'm saying is that it is not the most important factor. For so long we have seen our current situation from a one-dimensional perspective, when it is really much more complex than that. We assume that having more money is the answer.

But money doesn't change your fundamental makeup. Think of it this way: What if someone told you he would quit eating donuts once he got thin? The first thing you'd wonder is, how does he intend to get thin in the first place? Second, even if he did get thin, it's not as if this will magically create new habits, mind-sets, and behaviors—like removing a craving for donuts. From my own many failed attempts at joining a health club (because hey, if I join it, then I'll be motivated to work out), I know firsthand that this kind of thinking puts the cart before the horse.

31

Change Yourself, Not Your Income

My desire is that you experience real change—the kind of change that lasts beyond the time you spend reading this book. That kind of change is deep and internal; it starts inside you, right at the core of your beliefs about money and your relationship to it. You must open up to the idea that you played a role in creating your present situation. You need to embrace the truth that what's inside you is the key to the future you desire. It isn't a quick or easy process, but it is a lasting one. Once you change, you'll be amazed at the changes that happen around you. New beliefs, new vision, new habits, and new opportunities become possible.

If more money really were the main thing, wouldn't your financial woes have been resolved with your last pay raise or tax refund? No, the issues are too complex and interconnected to be fixed so easily. And if you focus too much on your own lack of money, it will keep you from noticing your overspending, underplanning, overborrowing, and undersaving behaviors that factor into your current situation. Left ignored, these harmful behaviors trump the benefit that comes from any windfall.

When you're tempted to think that one simple answer— more money—would change everything, remember this: It took hundreds of thousands of individual decisions for you to arrive where you are today. You'll only arrive in a better place when you have the ability to make decision upon decision that leads you in that new direction.

The Day Everything Changed for Me

Our first child was born in April 2007. She was healthy and so was I, and within days our family of three returned home.

I laid Victoria in her crib that first night, then crawled into bed myself. I prayed a silent prayer: "Dear Lord, what have I done? I am pee-my-pants scared. I don't know that I can take care of this child, but I think it's too late now to change my mind. Please help me because I have no idea what I'm doing. Help Marco too, so we don't kill each other in this process. Amen."

If you've ever brought a baby home from the hospital, then you know that feeling and may have prayed a similar prayer. It was the second time in my life I'd prayed that way. The first was when we decided to get out of debt. It may sound crazy to compare this decision with the responsibility that comes with having a baby, but changing your lifestyle in order to get out of debt is a big deal. For a few weeks Marco and I talked about the purpose of our lives. We'd come to see that our debt-ridden lifestyle was hindering us from accomplishing all we were created to do. It was a serious thing when we decided that we would get out of debt and never go back there again.

I agreed with the plan, but the next day I woke up with a sinking feeling in my stomach. That's when my silent prayers began. "Dear Lord, what have I done? I am pee-my-pants scared. I don't know that we can pay back everyone from whom we've borrowed and never borrow again. I know it's too late to change my mind now. Please help me because I have no idea what I'm doing. Help Marco too, so we don't kill each other in this process. Amen."

Financially, we'd been through a defining moment.

In an instant I accepted responsibility for my current financial situation *and* accepted the responsibility to change. All my life I'd believed that if I had more money, *then* things would change. Now here I was. I didn't have any more money, yet I had agreed to change. No more scapegoats. Sobering.

Becoming Responsible

Before I understood the things we are talking about here, I wanted someone or something else to change my financial life. As a college senior I met a bright young man who was part of the air force's Reserve Officer Training Corps. He would graduate with a stable military career ahead of him. He'd have a debt-free start too, courtesy of the air force paying his tuition and a solid North Dakota upbringing. From the time he was a six- or seven-year-old kid, he helped his parents farm their land. He learned to save and invest and developed an abhorrence for debt. He was the only person I knew at the time who had a nice car—a sporty one at that—and had paid cash for it. As a twenty-year-old college student. In every fathomable way he was financially responsible.

> *I don't have enough money to be able to change my financial life,*
>
> *became*
>
> *I have all the money it takes to establish my financial future.*

Me? Not so much. I was about to graduate with $20,000 in student loans (which was a lot in the 1990s) and no confidence in my ability to provide for myself. I'd seen my parents struggle to make ends meet. We lost my childhood home to foreclosure. My parents experienced bankruptcy. If they had a hard time financially, what made me think I could do any better? I wanted to marry this young man in part because I believed he'd rescue me financially. We didn't marry and I was never rescued.

I think about where I was as a young person and compare it to that of a roommate I had in my early twenties. She was part of the AmeriCorps VISTA program, which I always described as a domestic Peace Corps. She earned squat for pay. She had a living stipend that was well below minimum wage, and her agreement with the AmeriCorps VISTA program prohibited her from getting a second job. Her work was noble, but she made a small fraction of what I was making. At some point she had a financial need. Whether her car broke down or something else happened, I can't quite remember, but I remember her response: She told me she'd take money out of savings. I had nothing in savings, but here she had set money aside even while earning such a low wage. My friend didn't wait for better circumstances to happen to her before she got her financial act together. She knew she had chosen a low-paying volunteer position. She also knew that she had to create the future she wanted. She took responsibility.

That friend is living in the future she was creating back then. She and her husband own a variety of real estate. They recently paid cash for a new car. I wasn't surprised when she told me that, after being unemployed for nine months recently, she had *more* money in savings at the end of her unemployment than when she started. That's what happens when you live responsibly.

Choosing to Change

When I was single, my house was immaculate. Every morning I made my bed. Dishes were washed and put away immediately after every meal. Each of my belongings had a designated home, and everything always returned there when I was done using it. Now, as a mom with small kids, it's a different story. Marco and I constantly step over dolls, blocks, books, crayons, cars, and other toys I didn't even know we owned. Since I've had kids, I've experienced an exponential increase in my tolerance for a perpetual mess, with one exception—when we're expecting company.

When we'll be entertaining guests, everything changes, and I face the facts. I usually have a high tolerance for Rube Goldberg machines made out of toilet paper tubes, but I won't put up with them when friends or family are coming over.

Financially, today's the day company's coming over. What you once tolerated isn't tolerable anymore. Just like my family gets busy cleaning and dusting when we're preparing for company, it's time for you to take action.

Your actions start with a set of deliberate choices. When you choose to accept your past and your role in the present, you can walk into a different future. The largest challenge to accepting your past is forgiveness.

Woven into the backstory of our financial lives are setbacks, hurts, wounds, and missteps. We all have them. Sometimes we've hurt ourselves with our own addictive behavior, or we've lusted for things and given in to overspending. Sometimes those around us have made financial decisions that have directly impacted us. Our spouse or children may have pilfered away savings, stolen from us, or made unwise investments. Other times uncontrollable circumstances have dealt a blow to us financially—maybe it's a lost job, an accident, an illness, or a natural disaster. No matter the source, it's our responsibility to forgive ourselves or others so that we can move forward into a healthier financial life.

Years ago I felt locked in an emotional prison, angry with myself and others for a string of injustices. I'd hear pastors and others talk about forgiveness, but I never understood exactly *how* to forgive. Then I came across Neil Anderson's book *The Bondage Breaker.* In it, Anderson explains what

forgiveness is and why it is a starting point to personal trans-
formation. I'm living proof that he's right, even in the financial realm. Anderson explains forgiveness by saying,

> Forgiveness is not forgetting. . . . Forgetting may be the result
> of forgiveness, but it is never the means of forgiveness. When
> we bring up the past against others, we haven't forgiven them.
> Forgiveness is a choice, a crisis of the will. . . . But forgive-
> ness is difficult for us because it pulls against our concept of
> justice. We want revenge for offenses suffered. . . .
> **Forgiveness is agreeing to live with the consequences of
> another person's sin.** Forgiveness is costly; we pay the price
> of the evil we forgive. Yet you're going to live with those
> consequences whether you want to or not; your only choice
> is whether you will do so in the bitterness of unforgiveness
> or the freedom of forgiveness. (emphasis added) [4]

Today is the day to let go of your past and start focusing
on your future. To do this, make a list of everyone, including
yourself, that you need to forgive in order to accept your present financial situation. Feel free to list each individual offense
so you can release them from each and every one. Then you
need to make a painful choice. You need to choose to "bear
the burden of their offenses by not using the information
about their offenses against them again in the future."[5] This
is not about *feeling like* you want to forgive—it's a matter
of choice. Feelings may (or may not) follow this activity, but
you aren't seeking feelings. You are untying yourself from
the past. Your past has kept you from accepting your present situation and, therefore, being able to take the reins of
your future.

With your list in hand (and maybe a box of Kleenex if your
wounds are deep), it's time to make the following declaration

I have $_____ of debt. I am not a victim of debt. I have chosen to overspend, overborrow, and/or undersave. My choices have created my current situation. Others may have had a negative influence on me and my finances, but I chose to associate with them.

I choose to forgive myself for my history of poor choices. I also forgive _____ (insert names) for _____ (actions), which have negatively influenced my finances. I forgive myself for allowing someone else's negative influence into my life. By forgiving, I choose to accept the consequences of their actions.

Effective immediately, I choose to change. I choose to accept the consequences of the poor choices that I've made in the past, and I accept responsibility for my financial future. No longer am I waiting for someone or something to rescue me. I am taking steps to secure the future I want for myself. Now. I will learn what I need to know so that I can responsibly handle the money I have.

out loud. Through this, you are accepting personal responsibility for your financial situation, breaking the tie to "If only I had more money" thinking, and forgiving those who have negatively influenced you.

Quiz

Do you hold on to the false belief that having more money would solve your financial problems? Here's a quiz that may help reveal your own internal attitudes. Using the following chart, place a number after every statement.

1 = Never	2 = Rarely	3 = Sometimes	4 = Frequently	5 = Always

____ 1. I believe I have too little money left at the end of the month to save any of it.

___ 2. I don't believe I can provide for myself and my family financially.

___ 3. I play the lottery.

___ 4. I dream of getting a huge salary increase.

___ 5. I believe my current financial situation is not my fault.

___ 6. I set up my tax withholdings so I get a huge tax refund each year.

Tally your scores. Your total demonstrates how strongly you hold the attitude that more money would solve your financial problems.

0–10: This attitude has minimal influence on your financial decision making. Other attitudes may need addressing first.

11–20: This attitude is part of your financial decision-making process. For your long-term success it needs to be addressed.

21–30: This attitude strongly influences your financial decisions. It is a priority to change this attitude.

Discussion Questions

Here are a few questions to help you think through your financial situation, either by yourself or with a small group:

1. When describing your financial situation, where do you tend to assign responsibility? Are there people you need to forgive in order to move forward?

2. How were financial decisions handled in your household growing up?

3. What expectations did you have about the future when you were younger that haven't been met?

4. Do you know anyone who has a low income but seems to be doing well financially? If so, what decisions do you think they've made to create their current situation?

5. After reading this chapter, are there any beliefs you need to change about yourself or your money?

3

I deserve a treat

The longer range your vision, the better your decision.

—Pastor Mac Hammond

*W*hen Marco graduated from college in May 2006, it was cause to celebrate. See, he is a first-generation immigrant who arrived in the U.S. with $500 in his pocket, with limited English ability, and not knowing a soul. He came from Brazil to get a college education at an American university.

His path to accomplishing that dream had some road bumps. After getting a two-year degree at a community college in 1995, he went on to the local university. By day he drove a school bus and by night he studied. Then he experienced a divorce and some personal setbacks, then dropped out.

When I met him some eight years later, he still talked about his dream of getting a B.A. from an American university. Much to his surprise, it turns out that he needed only three additional classes to complete his program. We agreed that he'd take them during the 2005–2006 school year, and in May 2006 he walked across the stage and received his hard-earned diploma. It really was a dream come true for him.

For weeks leading up to graduation, Marco told me about his desire to buy a class ring. I agreed, in theory, that it would be nice to have one. I didn't agree on the timing. We had a trip to Brazil planned right after commencement. I felt financially stretched thin. I wanted him to delay the purchase.

On the afternoon that he was fitted for his graduation robe, I got an email from him at work. It read something like this:

Sweetie,

The coolest thing happened when I got fitted for my robe. They gave me a very nice frame for hanging my diploma on the wall. It has the school's name on it in gold, and the colors will match the décor in our living room.

Wow, that's great, I thought. He had also expressed a desire for a nice frame to hang his diploma, and I'm glad he was able to get the frame as a gift. But I was puzzled about why they were giving away frames. Maybe it was the school's gift to each graduate. Or maybe it was a gift from the international student society. Marco had said something about an award ceremony for international students. I settled myself on that idea and kept reading.

All I had to do to get the free frame was buy a class ring. So I did. I felt like I deserved it after having worked so hard for my degree. I'm excited for you to see the frame when you get home from work tonight.

Love you,
Marco

We're Justifying

When you hear the words *I deserve it* run through your mind, know this: You are justifying. You are being tempted to make an impulse purchase and need a justification in order to pull the trigger. It's an impulse decision driven by a desire for some sort of emotional fix.

Making decisions based on emotion is not bad. In fact, it's been scientifically proven that we *need* emotion to decide anything.[1] Without an emotional impetus in one direction or another, we'd experience constant paralysis by analysis. We'd endlessly spin, weighing pros and cons into eternity. Emotion is what tips the scale and causes us to choose one option over another.

I'm not talking about eliminating the emotional element from your spending—you need it. But I am going to talk about giving your emotions a different role in your decision making. Consider this example to illustrate the point.

A Classic Example

Jenny has had a rough day. Really, it's been a tough week. On Monday afternoon her boss said she was disappointed with the quality of Jenny's recent work. That caught Jenny off guard, since she's always been a high achiever. Then again, she and her husband haven't been getting along very well in recent months. It's like they can't agree on much of anything. There have always been issues between them, but their oldest daughter has gotten into trouble at school recently and the situation has highlighted their inability to communicate. When Jenny quiets down and is honest with herself, she's not too surprised that her work has been impacted. It is hard for

43

her to focus. She's been staying up late arguing with Brad, then worrying about her daughter and her own future when she lies down to fall asleep.

Finally, Friday comes. On her way to work she fills up with gas and gets a coffee and donut while she's there. On her way to the car she has a fleeting guilty thought about her coffee and donut purchase, reflecting on a recent conversation with Brad. Things have been tighter than normal financially since his overtime hours were cut. *It's an insignificant purchase,* she tells herself. *Plus, I deserve this pick-me-up at the end of such a crummy week.*

At lunchtime she steps out of the office and heads to the food court at a nearby mall. After a quick bite, she takes time to meander through her favorite department store, eyeing the new spring fashions. Her eye catches an adorable dress that she'd love to wear on Easter. She tries it on and, wow, it's a flattering number. Jenny smiles as she admires herself in the mirror. On a whim she decides to buy the sixty-five-dollar dress. Approaching the register, she has second thoughts about it, since she hadn't discussed the purchase with Brad. A voice inside her says, *You need something to wear on Easter anyway, Brad can't argue with that. Plus, it has been a tough week and this helps make up for it.* Deciding that those things are true, she charges the dress and heads back to work to finish out the week.

Why Do We Do It?

Let's look at what was going on with Jenny. Like many of us, she is in the midst of a life full of stressors and is faced with multiple disappointments. Handling stress and disappoint-ment is a complicated and multifaceted issue for everyone.

This chapter is not intended to oversimplify something that may have deep and strong roots in us; it is intended to show us how we translate stress, disappointment, and even accomplishments, like Marco's graduation, into justifications to impulse shop.

In our example, Jenny made a series of impulse purchases. Her goal at each step was to feel a little better about herself, her life, and her circumstances. The truth is, nothing she can buy—large or small—will change her marriage, her daughter, her job, or her life for the better and the long term. What does change as she spends on a whim is her own temporary emotional state and, therefore, her perception of the challenges before her.

Impulse buying releases a chemical in the brain called dopamine. Dopamine is responsible for pleasurable feelings. Dr. Gregory Berns, an Emory University neuroscientist and author of *Satisfaction: The Science of Finding True Fulfillment* (Henry Holt, 2005), calls the role of dopamine while shopping "a fuel injector for action."[2] A study of rats showed that when they were placed in new surroundings, they experienced higher levels of dopamine.[3] It's not surprising, then, that when we try on new clothes and buy things—large or very small—we experience a pleasure surge.

It isn't just the buying and trying on that release dopamine; the very anticipation of making a purchase causes dopamine to be released in the brain too. Thinking about buying something makes us feel good. In one study, Dr. Berns and his colleagues found that volunteers who had drops of Kool-Aid trickle onto their tongues in a random pattern had higher levels of dopamine than those who had drops trickle at predictable intervals. That study shows that the anticipation of an event—whether Kool-Aid drops, new shoes, or a mocha on the way in to the office—is almost always more climactic than the event itself.[4]

Back to Jenny and our story. As she got ready on Friday morning, she started thinking about picking up a treat at the gas station when she stopped to fill up. In her mind the thought sounded like this: *Jenny, you deserve a treat this morning.* As she embraced it, ruminated on it, and anticipated it, the dopamine levels surged. Long before she made that simple purchase, she had masked the pressure of her daily life with a dopamine surge.

Like any chemical or drug-induced high, it wears off. By lunchtime, when she heads to the mall, Jenny gets a new surge of the happy-making dopamine as she stands among the racks of beautiful spring-like merchandise. In the high of that moment, the thought of owning a dress that looks so good is irresistible to her. She felt good at the checkout, but by her drive home she was regretting her choice. That's not unusual, as almost every impulse purchase is a letdown, according to impulse-shopping expert Dr. Berns.[5]

Another Way to Get What We Want

Starting each January, Susan sets aside fifteen dollars per month to use toward new spring and summer clothes. She loves boating and being on the lake, so it's important to her that she have nice clothes to wear as she enjoys the water. She modestly saves, and just before Memorial Day she heads to the mall with seventy-five dollars in hand. Knowing she is on a budget, Susan has prioritized the new pieces she wants for the summer and is familiar with the sales at all the major stores. Susan and her daughter enjoy a leisurely day of trying on clothes, visiting, and scoring some great bargains. She's proud to come home with three new articles of clothing and a pair of earrings, plus two dollars and change to spare.

Susan starts her shopping experience *already* feeling good. Jenny, on the other hand, bought things *so that* she would feel good. When you feel angry, stressed, guilty, or bored, you need to be particularly watchful for this deceptive attitude. You may find yourself with thoughts like these:

- I've had a hard week; I deserve this.
- I worked so hard, I deserve a nice treat.
- If I could just take a break and get myself a treat, then I'll feel better.
- This treat will help me get through the day.

It's the impulsivity of this attitude that makes it dangerous. It destroys the best-laid budgets and convinces us to work against our long-term goals. Yes, this attitude also includes an element of entitlement thinking, which is something we cover in-depth in the chapter "I'll Fake It 'Til I Make It."

It's the Leaky Toilet

Imagine you open your water bill one month and find that it is sky high. Instantly you know that something, somewhere in your house has to be leaking. There is no way that you could rack up such a bill yourself, apart from a leak. If this happened to me, I'd start on a quest to find the leaky culprit. I'd check every faucet, every showerhead, every pipe until I found the problem's source. Then I'd set my mind to fixing it.

In this case, you discover a silent leaky toilet. It's not like it was running and you'd been ignoring it, but it was stealthily leaking day in and day out to the tune of a couple hundred bucks in this last water bill. Immediately you fix it. You see a huge decrease in your bill during the next cycle.

For Marco and me, I-deserve-a-treat purchases were the leaky toilet in our finances. We couldn't see exactly why we didn't have enough money. We couldn't pinpoint a single purchase that pushed us over budget and prompted us to carry a credit card balance. But all the while, money was leaking out of our life in two-dollar, five-dollar, and seven-dollar increments. We really believed that our treats of choice—a pumpkin muffin and hazelnut coffee for me and an iced tea and sandwich from the gas station cooler for Marco (yes, he really eats *and* enjoys those sandwiches)—weren't impacting us financially. I mean, no one pays the mortgage with a three-dollar coffee, right?

"Thank You, Caribou"

Shortly after we got serious about eliminating our debt, Marco had a breakthrough in his thinking about his treats. As a backdrop, you have to know that Marco has Attention Deficit Disorder (ADD). Impulse control is *really* challenging for those who have ADD. Although Marco has had ADD since childhood, he wasn't diagnosed until 2010. That means he was untreated for it while we got into debt and during the years we got out.

In the early days of getting out of debt, we built a weekly allowance for Marco into our monthly spending plan. It was our mutual acknowledgement that resisting impulse buys was hard for him—especially on bad days, hard days, and exceptionally good days. We created a place in our finances for him to indulge a bit and get his fix but not throw us off course. We allocated twenty dollars each week for him to spend however he'd like without having to answer to me for a dime of it. Typically he spent his twenty dollars at a coffee shop and bakery on mochas and croissants or on lunch out with those gas station sandwiches.

Marco started to get fed up with his habit and wondered if he could put that twenty dollars to use elsewhere in our lives. Without telling me, he quit buying his mochas and deli sandwiches and stashed his twenty-dollar bill. He kept this up for a few weeks and finally told me about it one Friday night. It came up when he suggested that we take an impromptu trip to beautiful northern Minnesota. "Maybe we could rent a cabin or something," he suggested. Prudent, non-spontaneous Carrie wasn't keen on the expense of an unplanned trip—even if it was just a single night away. Then Marco remembered his stash of twenty-dollar bills and pulled them out, exclaiming, "Hey, we can use this money that I've been saving!"

So we did. I went online and found a cabin on a lake within our price range. We packed our bags and hit the road. It was a wonderful four-hour drive, much of it weaving and winding through the gorgeous scenery of the Chippewa National Forest.

Our cabin had a stunning view of a lake, towering pines, and birch trees. Since it was off-season, we negotiated for their largest cabin at the price one normally pays for the smallest. It was peaceful and relaxing. We enjoyed some walks through the woods, quiet reading time, and sitting on the porch looking at the water.

At one point I was sitting on the couch reading (which is one of my favorite pastimes), and Marco came into the living room. In a singsong voice and almost twirling around, as if doing a silly dance, he started saying again and again, "Thank you, Caribou! Thank you, Caribou! Thank you, Caribou, for this cabin!" If you aren't familiar, Caribou Coffee is a Minneapolis-based coffee chain. It's the chain where Marco always bought his mocha.

Marco's declaration in that cabin was the moment he first realized that the money he spends on impulsive I-deserve-a-treat purchases could be used for larger, better, more satisfying things. Yes, he and I had talked plenty of times about how his four-dollar-per-day mocha habit required us to set aside eighty dollars per month for him. Talking about eighty dollars per month was not nearly as powerful as experiencing something that eighty dollars could buy.

That very day in that cabin Marco changed his mind. He replaced "I deserve a treat" with a phrase we use to this day— "I work too hard for my money." It was the day we decided to start plugging the leaky toilet in our finances.

Creating a Larger Context

I love jigsaw puzzles. My mom and her family love jigsaw puzzles. I remember spending hours (maybe it was just a few minutes, but it seemed like hours) at the table with my grandmother. First we would empty the pieces from the box and turn them all right side up. Then we'd display the puzzle's box top somewhere on the table so we could see what the completed image our thousand pieces would create. Then we'd assemble the exterior frame—corners first, since those were easiest—and go to work on the interior of the puzzle.

My grandmother's puzzles weren't meant for kids. They were thousand-piece images of fall foliage where every. single. piece. of the puzzle contained similar shades of red, gold, and brown. Our saving grace was the box top. We'd find a piece, then examine the completed image on that box top, looking for where the piece fit. That was especially critical with the first pieces we put in place. As we completed more and more of the puzzle we could make judgments based on our work, but the box top was all we had to start with.

In our financial lives we need a jigsaw puzzle box top too. For Marco, an overnight at a cabin resort was a box top. Prior to that weekend, he'd seen his simple indulgences as insignificant to our overall financial goals. When he realized that foregoing those indulgences could create something much larger—like a thousand little cardboard puzzle pieces fitting together to make one beautiful image—he realized that seemingly small insignificant financial decisions can compound into something meaningful.

Our entire story of getting out of debt is a story about the power of creating a larger context. Creating a budget, tracking our spending, and living within our means were not new concepts to Marco and me in 2006. I'd gone through some financial literacy–type courses, and a marriage class we attended talked extensively about how to operate family finances in a healthy way. We'd heard all these things but didn't put them into practice in our life until June 2006, because we didn't have a reason larger than ourselves to do it until then. We had a desire to move to Brazil.

During a trip to Rio de Janeiro in May 2006, Marco and I dreamed of a life where we could move to Brazil one day. Our finances were a huge roadblock to the fulfillment of that dream. Brazil is primarily a cash-based society. People pay cash for cars and houses and big-ticket items. We couldn't get to the end of a month without our credit card, let alone pay cash for a car. That seemed a million miles away.

We got introspective. Did we want the life we had? Did we want the debt we were carrying? The cost of that life and that debt was tremendous. It meant that living in Brazil would never be an option for us. Or we could adjust ourselves, pay off the debt we had, learn to stay out of debt, and start saving money for things we'd need. If we did that, then one day we could move to Brazil and fulfill that dream.

Our desire to move to Brazil created a new frame, a new lens through which we looked at all our financial decisions. Suddenly every decision had meaning. Suddenly the sum of the parts was larger than the whole. Suddenly we had a deep and lasting motivation to actually *do* the things we'd known to do all along. All we had to ask ourselves was "Which do I want more?"

Creating a Positive Frame

Now we understand what lies underneath I-deserve-a-treat thinking. There's a component of entitlement, which we'll discuss more, and an element of impulsivity and an emotional thrill at the point of purchase. We've learned that there is a bona fide physiological reason we get an emotional kick from shopping and buying, albeit short-lived. One way to rein in these impulsive purchases is to create a larger-than-ourselves goal or dream to remind us of why we are foregoing our impulsive treats.

There are as many unique goals, dreams, or as I call them "frames" as there are readers of this book. But each one will fall into one of two camps. It will be gain oriented or focused on pain avoidance. Think about what this might look like where weight loss is concerned.

If you struggle with your weight, you might set out to lose thirty pounds. You could decide that your afternoon treat from the vending machine is your problem and decide to give that up. Those are loss-based goals and will be met with minimal results.

In fact, I'm pretty sure that if you decide to give up an afternoon snack and don't frame it within something positive, something you hope to gain as a result, you'll experience junk food cravings like never before. All your mind will have to think about is the junk food. Yes, you want to avoid it, but like a broken record your mind will play and replay an image of the thing you want to give up. Playing that image over and over will stir a desire in you, and that desire will eventually become unbearable and you'll yield to the temptation.

Instead, what if you set out to lose thirty pounds so you're comfortable wearing a swimsuit on an upcoming vacation? You'd have to give up your afternoon junk food snack as a step in that process. Certainly you'll think about a chocolate bar at 2:00 p.m., just like you have every day for the last six years. But this time you'll replace the thought of the candy bar with the thought of sunning on a beach with your family. Your resilience to the temptation will be stronger.

Your gain-oriented goal—beach and swimming time with your family in St. Thomas—supplants the short-term craving. It's not hard to cultivate a stronger desire for the larger goal than the short-term desire you're currently facing. If you lacked the ability to overcome the temptation simply by replacing the thought of junk food with the thought of the beach, you could take things further. You could put a Caribbean screensaver on your computer. You could read travel books about your destination and generate a positive expectancy for the trip. You could go so far as to tape a picture of your it's-a-smaller-size-than-what-I-wear-right-now swimsuit to the vending machine. (Your co-workers might have some questions about this one, though.) So even if all the other imagery failed, you'd look at that goal, the thing you hoped to gain, in the seconds before you chose to sabotage that future for a short-term thrill.

The statements have to be positive because we're inherently created to desire. Goals stated in the negative are often focused on suppressing behavior, dwelling on things we want to avoid: "I will no longer do x, y, or z." We have an insatiable need to desire, whether we use it for good or bad. When our goals are stated in the positive—how we will participate in the future, not what we will avoid—then we put that desire to work.

Your New Financial Frame

It is exactly the same thing with our finances. For my family, we had a huge goal of moving to Latin America one day. That goal was almost too lofty for my husband until he experienced the short-term win with the overnight at the cabin. Your charge right now is to create a new frame of reference for yourself. The possibilities are endless:

- Having a larger house so that your kids can play safely in the yard
- Becoming self-employed at the thing you'd love to do
- Providing a private school education for your kids so that the values you teach at home are reinforced by other adults in their lives
- Giving generously to a charity that's near and dear to your heart so it can extend mercy and compassion on others

In the first pass of creating a larger context, you might initially brainstorm loss-focused, pain-avoidance-type goals:

- Having debt collectors stop calling
- Averting foreclosure
- Avoiding divorce caused by constant fighting about money

Don't be discouraged if your initial thoughts are negative statements. Turn them around into something positive. Those same examples I made above could be turned around into these positive statements:

- Enjoying hearing the phone ring, knowing it is a friend or family member calling
- Providing a stable environment for my kids so that they can remain in their school
- Experiencing peaceful, respectful communication with my spouse about money that draws us closer together

These statements are the flip side of a negative coin. It's imperative that our new frame be positive because we have an incredible ability to tolerate pain. Think about parents who motivate their kids by yelling at them. Over time they need to yell louder and louder to garner the same result from the child. That's because the youngster learns to tolerate the pain of yelling, and over time, higher doses of pain are needed to generate the same level of motivation. You don't want to require an increasing amount of financial pressure to motivate you toward good choices.

Start with lofty life ambitions that seem beyond your reach today. Then step back into your current situation and create some midterm goals that can be achieved in the days and weeks ahead.

If You Don't Know Where to Start

If you're not sure where to start or can't imagine anything positive for your future, there is hope for you. I am confident that you have desires within you. They may be buried deep, but they are there. With a time of thoughtful cultivation, I believe you will uncover long-lost passions, interests, hopes, and ambitions. Those things—even if they seem fanciful at the moment—are the seeds of your new frame of reference.

To unearth these seeds, think back to times in your life when you were enjoying yourself. Times when you felt alive. Times when you felt passionate about something. Times when you experienced deep satisfaction. These times may not have been prolonged seasons but rather just fleeting moments, afternoons off, or long weekends. I believe you've had those moments.

I remember a time when a friend of mine was longing for a glimpse into her future. She was in a place that felt meaningless. She longed for a larger-than-herself goal, but she couldn't conjure up a single one. Then she did some soul searching and asked herself questions like these:

- What do I love to do?
- When have I felt fully alive?
- If money were no object, how would I spend my time?
- What talents or abilities do I have that I can use to bless those around me?
- When I want to relax, what do I do?
- If I were to plan the perfect week—vocationally, recreationally, spiritually, and in every other way—what components would it include?
- Who do I enjoy being with?

Over time she thought, prayed, journaled, and talked with close friends and family. She came to realize that the thing she loved and enjoyed the most in life was being outdoors. She loved camping, canoeing, rock climbing, hiking, backpacking, and every other high-adventure outdoor activity. But she wondered how a desire to be outdoors could translate into any sort of life goal. She compared herself and her desire with others' life desires and felt inferior. While others may want to be stay-at-home moms or advance in their careers, she loved nature and the woods.

After she took some time to think about it, a solution did begin to take shape. My friend imagined how satisfying life would be if she could run an adventure camp for kids. This wouldn't be a typical summer camp with crafts and "Kumbayah." She imagined running a camp that would take city kids, who normally don't get to experience the great outdoors, on week-long canoe trips, difficult hikes, or backpacking in mountain ranges so that they could experience the majesty of nature and also feel the accomplishment of performing the physical feats involved with the activities.

It had crystallized. My friend decided that one of her dreams in life was to run an outdoor adventure camp, so she pursued a master's degree in outdoor education and gained volunteer experience at a relevant nonprofit.

My point is this: You do have interests, passions, and desires within you. At first blush they may seem silly, trivial, or meaningless. Don't dismiss them. Cultivate them. Think about them. Develop them into a dream. Then keep that dream in front of you for the next time you're tempted to short-circuit it with frivolous spending justified by I-deserve-a-treat thinking.

Quiz

Do you frequently spend money on things you didn't plan to buy because you feel you deserve a treat? Here's a quiz that may help reveal your own internal attitudes. Using the following chart, place a number after every statement.

1 = Never	2 = Rarely	3 = Sometimes	4 = Frequently	5 = Always

1. When I'm having a hard day, a special treat feels more justified than on a typical day.
2. I believe that I may never get out of my current financial situation, so I might as well enjoy the small things in life.
3. I work hard for my money, so I deserve a latte/round of golf/new dress/new shoes a couple times a month.
4. I pay attention to the big expenses so I don't really need to worry about smaller purchases, even if they're unplanned.

Tally your scores. Your total demonstrates how strongly you hold the attitude that you "deserve it."

0–6: This attitude has minimal influence on your financial decision making. Other attitudes may need addressing first.

7–13: This attitude is part of your financial decision-making process. For your long-term success it needs to be addressed.

14–20: This attitude strongly influences your financial decisions. It is a priority to change this attitude.

Discussion Questions

Here are a few questions to help you think through your own financial situation, by yourself or with a small group:

1. Do you have particular treats that you turn to in order to get through a stressful day? Write them down.

2. When do you find yourself most tempted to get a treat?

3. Go through the list of questions that my friend who was longing for that glimpse into her future asked herself, taking some time to really think about your answers and perhaps asking for input from the people who know you best.

4. What is a big-picture goal you have that would require you to be in a different financial situation?

5. How can you turn your craving for treats into a craving for your bigger picture?

4

it won't happen to me

What is important is seldom urgent and what is urgent is
seldom important.

—President Dwight D. Eisenhower

Who doesn't love payday? Early in our marriage Marco
got a paycheck every Friday, and I got a direct deposit
every other week. I considered myself a diligent financial planner and a fiscally responsible person. Each payday
I would assess our current financial situation, look ahead at
the next two to four weeks, and make plans.

My high-tech accounting system was done on the back
of an envelope. I would start by balancing the checkbook.
I'd get the current balance from the bank's phone line, since
this was pre-Internet banking, then try to remember any
outstanding charges or checks that would be clearing soon.
From there I'd subtract out the bills and debt payments we
needed to make within the next pay period or two. Then I'd

allocate money for things like gas, groceries, and eating out. If there was anything left over, and there frequently was a little something left, then Marco and I would make decisions on a case-by-case basis about how to spend it.

I felt very proud of the planning I was doing for our family. I purposed to look *two* pay periods ahead when anticipating our expenses. I'd heard of the dangers of living paycheck to paycheck and deemed two paychecks to be a much healthier amount of foresight. I believed we budgeted our expenses and was convinced that we were living within our means.

As proud as I felt, I was also confused. We couldn't have money left over at the end of the month *and* be financially overextended, could we? All of our monthly bills were paid on time, but when something more significant came up—like a broken tooth that needed a crown or a fender bender with a $1,000 insurance deductible—*gulp!* We never seemed to have enough to cover those extra expenses. We also had an increasing debt load. Why were we turning to credit cards and other types of borrowing if we truly had more than enough? I couldn't make sense of it. It was an oxymoron. In our life, excess coexisted alongside lack.

Why the Oxymoron?

Marco and I only budgeted for the expenses that were in our face at the moment. We managed our money as if predictable and inevitable yet unscheduled things like birthday gifts and new shoes—and life's bona fide emergencies—wouldn't happen to us. We were living a lie. If it was March, I was not thinking about Christmas. When he was feeling strong and healthy, I was not planning for Marco to think he was having a heart attack, therefore needing an ER visit and extensive lab tests. If the furnace was working, I was not saving for its repair. We did not think about the future until the future came crashing into the present.

It's like a single mom I know. She has five kids and drives a school bus for a living. Last January she posted a Facebook status update that read something like "I just got my heating bill and can't believe how high it is. Better start pinching pennies." We live in Minnesota, where winters are frigid and ginormous heating bills are typical in December and January (and even in February and March in bad years). A cold winter (or high heating bill) is never really unexpected.

I myself have complained many times when a large car-repair bill seemed to pop up out of nowhere. I never specifically considered that on my way to work I pass through at least fifteen stop signs and traffic lights. Taking the same route home, I brake again for those fifteen-plus traffic signals. That means that every single workday I am thirty traffic signals closer to needing new brakes. New brakes were not an inevitable reality to me but rather something out of sight and out of mind. So instead of being ready to pay for car repairs when I needed them, I'd act flabbergasted and mad at the mechanic who delivered the message that my brakes would brake no more.

Based on my actions, you might suspect that I don't value a well-maintained, properly running car. Or you could think that my friend doesn't value a warm home on a cold January night. No. Not at all. It's just that my financial planning was disconnected from my values.

Be Led By a Compass

In the mid-1980s, the fourth graders at Birch Grove Elementary had a rite of passage. Every year they went on a long-anticipated winter field trip to a nature center and park preserve. The day away from school consisted of cross-country skiing, identifying animal tracks, heating canned soup over a campfire, and the highlight—orienteering.

In small groups we were given a compass and a set of coordinates, then charged to find our way through the deep, thick forest (well, it wasn't really too deep and thick, but it seemed that way to my nine-year-old eyes). When we found the tree at the end of each set of coordinates, we could ink a stamp on our tagboard passports to prove we'd been there. Group after group returned to the warming house with dramatic stories of finding their way from coordinate to coordinate simply by following their compass's guidance even when they couldn't see the next specially marked tree with their eyes. We were all amazed at the compass's ability to provide direction and our ability to follow that leading.

Instead of directing our financial course with a blind it-won't-happen-to-me attitude, we could operate like the orienteering nine-year-olds. We can use a compass, established by our personal values, to set our course, then allow that compass to guide us from financial goal to goal in the same way we went from tree to tree. This way, our financial priorities would reflect our values.

When we aren't led by a compass, the results can be deadly. October 24, 2004, was a horrific day in NASCAR history. En route to a race in Martinsville, Virginia, the Hendrick Motorsports aircraft crashed, killing all ten passengers, including Ricky Hendrick and former NASCAR driver John Hendrick.[1]

The National Transportation Safety Board (NTSB) investigated the crash and uncovered the cause: faulty navigation caused by human error. In foggy conditions, the plane missed its first landing attempt, then veered off course and crashed.

The NTSB says the pilot did not use all available navigational aids while attempting to land the plane.[2]

I am sad to hear of the loss of ten lives in an avoidable accident. The pilot, the one charged with steering the aircraft, had navigational instruments available to him but for some reason did not use those aids. The result was devastating.

In our financial lives, we have a navigational device available to us. Yes, we need a vision that is larger than ourselves to create a context for sound decision making—like we discussed in chapter 3. But we need even more than that. On a day-to-day basis, we need input that allows us to steer even in foggy conditions. Goals that flow out of clearly articulated values are our compass.

Four Types of Financial Priorities

Stephen Covey popularized the Eisenhower method of time management in his book *First Things First* (Simon & Schuster UK, 1994). In it he explains that effective time management evaluates every task through the lens of whether the task is important or not important, and whether it is urgent or not urgent. Every task falls into one of four quadrants, or types of tasks.

I believe the concept of considering something's urgency and importance translates into our personal finances. That framework creates four types of financial priorities, each one defined by its position along the urgent/not urgent and important/not important continuums.

Bills

As I described above, Marco and I lived almost exclusively in this category. We focused on what was urgent and

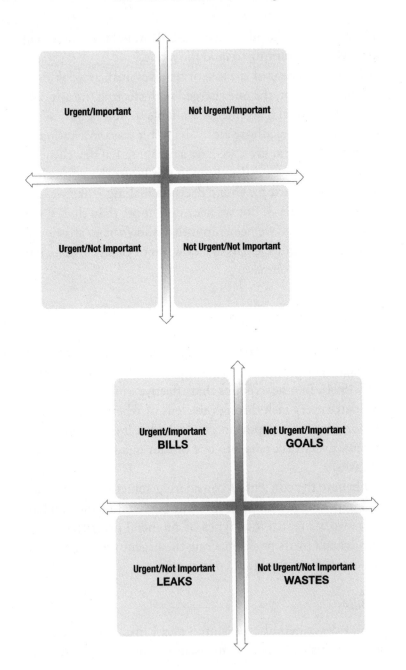

immediately before us. Many of the things in this category are essential to survival and to meeting life's basic needs. They truly are important, but they should not consume the entirety of our financial resources and focus. This category includes

- House payment/rent
- Utilities
- Insurance payments
- Groceries
- Gasoline to get to and from work
- Debt payments

Leaks

We extensively discussed financial leaks in chapter 3. These are right-now, in-your-face impulse buys that are not important. These expenses aren't aligned with your long-term dream and vision for your family. They are misaligned with your values and intended to give you a short-term emotional fix.

To be clear, I'm not picking on any particular expense. I'm talking about motive, which cannot be judged from the outside looking in. For example, you may grab lunch out with a co-worker and it's a leak. To someone else who has established a personal goal of creating stronger relationships with co-workers, it isn't a leak. Then lunch out is a planned and perfect way to make progress. But really, it isn't the actual expense or activity that matters; it's whether that item is consistent with your values, moving you toward your goals, and planned for.

Until Marco and I got serious about changing our financial situation, we spent 90 to 110 percent of our monthly income on some combination of bills and leaks. It left almost nothing for the most important category—goals.

Goals

Most every notable expense that you are thinking about for next month, six months from now, or next year falls into this category. These expenses are not urgent—they don't have to be paid today—but they are important to you, regardless of it being a need like a new roof on your house, or a want or desire like a much-needed vacation or a remodeling project at home. Usually these non-urgent expenses reflect some type of personal goal, whether you've consciously stated them that way or not.

Expenses in this category include items that are applicable to almost all of us:

- Christmas gifts (the goal may be to get gifts for all the kids and grandkids)
- New brakes for the car (the goal may be to drive reliable cars)
- New clothes for growing kids (the goal may be to have neat and clean kids)
- Supplies for maintaining the lawn (the goal may be to relax on summer nights by gardening)
- Medical and dental expenses (the goal may be to live long, healthy, comfortable lives)

Important but not urgent expenses are not limited to these generally applicable items. As you and your family establish unique personal goals—whether it is a remodeling project, vacations, sending a child to a specific summer camp, or upgrading to a nicer vehicle—you have your own goals that are birthed from your value set.

Most every one of those value-based goals costs something to accomplish. You can plan financially for those goals instead of waiting for them to become urgent expenses that upset the apple cart of your monthly bills. When we don't properly plan for the things that are coming six to twelve months from now, we are often left unprepared and turn to a credit card or other form of debt.

Wastes

In time management, the non-urgent and non-important items are considered distractions. Financially, I call them wastes. They are expenses that are more than grossly misaligned with our visions, goals, and values. They have a destructive component that actually works against the priorities we've otherwise set.

Addictions are the foremost wastes in my mind. My extended family has loved ones who have battled gambling addictions. It's not only costly in terms of dollars and cents, but it clouds the addict's judgment and makes healthy prioritizing difficult. Gambling is certainly not the only addiction. It may be alcohol, drugs, pornography, food, or shopping. These expenses are beyond a dripping leak. Left unresolved, they can derail the entire train.

Getting Your Goals in Place

By the end of this chapter I want you to have articulated value-based goals that you can use in your financial planning. Value-based goals move you away from it-won't-happen-to-me thinking. Instead of pretending that the future is not going to happen, you plan to create a future you want by setting goals, then moving toward those established benchmarks.

These benchmarks will guide your spending, your savings, and your relationship to debt as they reflect the non-urgent but important things in your life.

Our First Two Goals

When Marco and I decided that we would plan for our future, we immediately set two goals. The first was to get out of debt. The second goal was to stay out of debt for the rest of our lives. Those goals overshadowed all the other smaller ones, and still do.

We knew that meant we'd have to pay off all our current obligations and simultaneously save money so that we'd have enough to cover every future expense. We'd never been dili-

To avoid debt, you have to save money in advance of needing to spend it.

gent savers, so our process started by looking at the two types of expenses we knew we'd encounter in the weeks and months ahead—bona fide emergencies and planned expenses related to accomplishing our goals.

We learned the value of an emergency fund on Christmas morning, 2006. We got a phone call at 4:30 a.m.

that Marco's father had passed away. The funeral was being held the next day, so Marco had to get on a plane to Rio de Janeiro, Brazil, on Christmas Day. The ticket alone cost an insane amount—over $2,000—plus Marco had to take a week of unpaid time off to accommodate the trip. Thankfully, because we'd been building our emergency fund for about six months at that point, we buffered all those expenses without missing a financial beat. It was the first time we'd ever done that without credit cards. (It felt *really* good, in case you were wondering.) In chapter 10 I'll provide details of how to build your own emergency fund.

Your Goal List

Apart from unpredictable emergencies, you have goals, plans, desires, and ambitions for things you hope to do and buy. You need to make a list of everything you want or will need to spend money on in the next six to twelve months. Make this a raw, unedited list that isn't censored by self-talk that says "It's too big of a goal or too expensive—don't write it down." In my experience, suppressing a desire for something does not make the desire go away. What typically happens is you find a way to meet that desire outside of your established plan, and it creates financial pressure because it isn't planned for.

Trust me: It's better to put every single desire and need on your list so you can make choices to accommodate as many of them as possible. I've been surprised time and again with how many things Marco and I have been able to accomplish with intentional proactive planning. I am confident you can accomplish more than you ever imagined possible if you are completely honest with yourself and your spouse.

Think through these different categories and jot down a list of likely or desired expenses.

- **People.** Who is important to you? What will they need in the next few months? Gifts? New clothes, shoes, equipment? Other financial support?
- **Events.** Which holidays do you celebrate? What kinds of social gatherings will you attend or host? Think about the events associated with each family member's work, school, and groups like Scouts and youth groups.

- **Medical and dental.** What medical and dental procedures and equipment can you anticipate each family member needing this year, including eyeglasses, contacts, braces, and prescriptions?
- **Maintenance, repair, and replacement.** Which items do you own that need some sort of ongoing maintenance, repair, or cleaning? Is anything on its last leg, needing to be replaced soon?
- **Non-monthly bills.** Do you pay any utilities, subscriptions, dues, or other bills quarterly, semiannually, or annually?
- **Entertainment, vacation, and recreation.** Where do you plan to travel this year? What concerts, shows, and events will you buy tickets for? What does your family do for fun? Are there summer camps or weekend getaways to plan for?

Paring Back Your List

Now you have a laundry list of wants and needs. Your next step is to assign each one a dollar value and convert them into financial goals. "Save $750 to buy Christmas presents for my kids, nieces, and nephews next year" could become a goal on your list. If you quantify each item on the list, I suspect you'll run into a problem. You'll likely find that the total cost of fulfilling all your needs and wants is *greater* than your available income.

You have three choices at this point: You can incur debt so that you can spend beyond what you make; you can increase your income to cover those expenses; you can decrease your expenses to fit within your income.

I'm hopeful that before you made this list, you decided to avoid future debt. That leaves you to either increase income or decrease your expenses. Before you roll your eyes at me, sigh, and think, *I hate lists like this because I know I can't ever do the things I want. The things I need take up too much of my money,* hear me out. Before you start hunting for a moonlighting gig, let's see if you can find a different way. Maybe, just maybe, you can rework your list, provide for the things you value most, but do it in ways that cost less than what you're thinking they'd cost right now.

First Why, Then What

It is important to separate your goal from the value that's fueling it, because there is always more than one way to accomplish something—and some ways cost less than others. You may really want a new deck. You're ready to take out a home equity line of credit to get it built. Your husband disagrees with you and the topic has become a source of tension between you. After reading these words, you stop and think about why you want that new deck and why you want it this summer. Why aren't you willing to wait a year or two until you have the money saved?

> *What you want is your goal. Why you want it reflects your values.*

You realize two things when you get quiet and honest with yourself. First, you love entertaining and want an outdoor space where you can do it. Second, your sister recently redid her backyard and you love her space. You've put pressure on yourself to keep up with her. Once you identify that internal pressure, you let that go. You don't want to make financial decisions based on an unhealthy competitive drive. But your desire to entertain outdoors is real and legitimate.

73

Now you go back to your husband and instead of trying to convince him that you need a new deck, you share your desire to do more entertaining and explain why your current setup doesn't work as well as you'd like. He can see and understand what you're saying, since the two of you have hosted more parties, reunions, and gatherings over the years than he can count.

So you ask him, "Honey, can we think of four or five different ways we could meet my desire (to entertain outdoors) *this* summer while we also save for the deck I ultimately want?" The two of you brainstorm a handful of ideas, talk through the financial component of each, and devise a plan. This year you'll buy an outdoor rug and a new umbrella for your patio furniture without incurring any debt. With those two things, you are more comfortable utilizing the deck you have. (Plus, as an added bonus, you've eliminated "arguing about the deck" from your list of marital issues.)

Now it's time for you to go through your entire laundry list of goals and upcoming expenses to articulate the "why" behind each one. What is your motivation in desiring that thing? Why have you allocated that specific dollar amount for the item?

Let's use our example goal to save $750 to buy Christmas presents for your kids, nieces, and nephews next year. Why are you buying Christmas gifts for each of those people? You like to bless your children and enjoy seeing the look on their faces when they get gifts they've desired. You give to your nieces and nephews because your siblings give to your kids. You actually feel obligated to do it.

After talking with your siblings, you all agree that buying gifts for every kid is a financial burden, so you collectively decide to draw names and give one child a $25 gift. That saves you about $250 in Christmas gifts this next year. You are able to do what's most important to you—make your own kids smile—and spend less than what you had expected.

Communicating About Values

Right now in our life we have a lot of competing financial priorities. We recently bought a new-to-us home (yes, we took out a mortgage, but we have a goal and plan to pay it off in no more than fourteen years), and off the top of my head I can list a dozen things we need or want for our new house, including a storage shed, a new water heater, blinds for all the windows, a snowblower, a new central air-conditioning unit, and on and on and on.

The house isn't the only thing we expect to spend money on in upcoming months. We'd like to take a family vacation this summer. We typically go to a friend's cabin up north, but we would like to take our girls on a trip outside of Minnesota this year. Our oldest starts kindergarten in the fall. Her school requires a very specific uniform, so outfitting her will be a $300 to $400 proposition. Marco has a medical procedure he's been waiting to have done that will cost nearly $1,000. We could use a few more sets of bed sheets—one for each bed in our house, since they've gotten tattered lately. Not to mention that we put almost $10,000 into our old house before we sold it, so we'd love to replenish our savings.

Big and small, we experience constant demands for our money. Sometimes it seems that when Marco and I look ahead to plan and discuss what's coming, the list of goals super-exceeds our budget. In those times, it often happens that Marco and I don't immediately agree on which goals should get financial priority and which ones get delayed for a few months. Compounding the problem is my opinionated and stubborn nature that can drown out Marco's attempts to express viewpoints that differ from mine.

Choose From Two

Like the woman who wanted a new deck and found herself consistently arguing with her husband about it, we have found that when we shift the conversation from *what* we want to *why* we want something, the tension diffuses. Time and again we've used a simple technique to facilitate this type of values-focused dialogue. I call it "Choose From Two." It's especially useful when Marco and I have a long list of competing priorities.

We make a laundry list of goals. Our list includes everything we could want or imagine spending money on or saving money for in the months ahead. Usually we're in sync about the priority of some things on the list but disagree about other items. We take one of the contentious items and compare it to one other thing on the list. We each have to answer these questions about those two items:

- Which of these two items is more important to you? Which one do you want more or do you want first?
- Why?

Then we line that same contentious item up against the next thing on the list. We ask the questions again for those two items. We continue through the list, comparing the contentious item with each other thing and repeating the questions for each pair. Then we move to the next contentious item and repeat the entire process.

76

Through this choose-from-two exercise, we hear each other's reasoning. I understand why he wants to spend or save for certain things, and he understands that from me. Then we can develop a plan that meets the most important needs, but does it in ways that are potentially different from what either of us first expected.

Yesterday a friend told me about a conversation she and her husband had. He really wanted to take a summer vacation to a certain city; she really didn't want to. After she asked him why he wanted the vacation, he explained that a vacation is the primary way he unplugs and relaxes from his busy life as a lawyer. It's how his dad disconnected from work when he was a child and he cherishes those memories. He wanted to go to that particular city because it is a place my friend and her husband had not been together as a couple. She resisted the idea mainly because she wanted a less expensive vacation so they could also get a new kitchen table, which is something they desperately need. They eventually agreed upon an alternate destination that will provide him the break and vacation he desires while costing less so she can also get the kitchen table she wants.

Protecting Me From Me

After Marco and I made our first set of financial goals, including a commitment to build a three- to six-month emergency fund, we had to start saving money toward them. This petrified me, as I knew that I was a threat to our success.

A few years prior, I'd sold a home I owned for a $70,000 profit. Yes, you read that correctly—$70,000. I paid off the remainder of my student loans and my car loan, then gave a significant cash donation to my church. I was out of debt and had $25,000 in savings.

That was the same time I moved to the Peruvian Amazon, where I lived and worked as a missionary for a year. I had financial partners who gave contributions toward my $1,000 monthly living stipend. Considering that my housekeeper, who worked six days per week, made less than $100 per month, $1,000 is a huge amount in that part of the world.

But it wasn't enough for me. I didn't see myself as limited to my monthly stipend. I considered my savings account to be an extension of my checking account and readily transferred money as I needed it. I put on large ministry events, bought the local church a variety of things, and outfitted the three-bedroom home I rented (and lived in by myself) with furniture and appliances. When I returned to the states after a year, I had less than $1,000 in that savings account.

Now that Marco and I had set financial goals, I knew that we had to minimize the possibility for me to sabotage our savings. Marco and I both knew that if we did not actually save the money we'd earmarked for our goals, we'd continue to live as if "it won't happen to me." We would not be able to get out and stay out of debt. We did two things:

- **We automated the deposits into our savings account.** I could not be trusted to manually move the money each month. ACH transfers are like direct deposits that can be initiated or cancelled only by completing paperwork at a bank branch. This forced us to prioritize saving because if we didn't have enough to cover the ACH transfer, then we'd be charged an overdraft fee.
- **We made withdrawing money difficult.** We put our savings account in a new bank that did not allow online transfers back into our checking account. We did not initially get debit cards or an ATM card for the account.

We only had a checkbook (and not very many places take checks nowadays), or we had to physically go to the bank and withdraw money. To make it even more difficult for us, we intentionally chose a small bank with limited hours and very few branch locations.

Protecting You From You

Now it's time for you to take an honest look in the mirror at your track record of saving money.

- Do you have a positive track record of saving money?
- Have you experienced a glass ceiling that your savings balance has not been able to exceed?
- Are you able to successfully make regular deposits in the full amount you intended?
- Do you view your savings account as an extension of your checking account?
- Do you make withdrawals for things other than what the money is being saved for?

If you have any sabotaging tendencies, identify what they are. Think about why they exist, then make a plan to defend yourself from them. You need to be able to actually save money—large sums of money—if you are going to accomplish your life's goals without constant financial pressure.

Quiz

Do you often have expenses come up that surprise and frustrate you? Here's a quiz that may help reveal your own internal attitudes. Using the following chart, place a number after every statement.

1 = Never	2 = Rarely	3 = Sometimes	4 = Frequently	5 = Always

1. I use my credit cards for emergencies and unexpected expenses.
2. Every time I try to set money aside, I pull it back out of savings.
3. There's no way I can save for emergencies or expenses outside of my monthly bills, so I prefer to not think about them.
4. I live in fear of my financial future.

Tally your scores. Your total demonstrates how strongly you hold the attitude that "surprise" expenses are indeed surprises.

> 0–6: This attitude has minimal influence on your financial decision making. Other attitudes may need addressing first.

> 7–13: This attitude is part of your financial decision-making process. For your long-term success it needs to be addressed.

> 14–20: This attitude strongly influences your financial decisions. It is a priority to change this attitude.

Discussion Questions

Here are a few questions to help you think through your own financial situation, by yourself or with a small group:

1. Make your uncensored list of everything you will need or *want* to spend money on in the next six to twelve months, using the suggestions on pages 71–72 to trigger your thinking. If you are married, make separate lists.

2. Now that you have your list of "whats," talk about your "why" for each item. Listen to yourself and your spouse without judgment.

3. Prioritize your list. If necessary, use the choose-from-two method.

4. What are some creative ways you can satisfy your "why" without spending as much money as you initially expected?

5. Identify, write down, and share with your group any sabotaging tendencies you can identify in yourself. What steps would work for you to defend yourself?

5

I'll fake it 'til I make it

If you love money, you will never be satisfied;
if you long to be rich, you will never get all you want.

—Ecclesiastes 5:10

*A*few years after Marco and I were married, we needed to replace one of our vehicles. Both our cars were older but paid for. We knew we'd finance our new car, so we started by figuring out what we could afford in a monthly payment. The payments translated into a $15,000 to $17,000 vehicle.

The car we were keeping was a Toyota Camry. We really liked it and decided to focus our attention on Camrys. There were plenty of them in our price range. Somehow, though, we started to entertain the idea of a Toyota Avalon. The Avalon is a step up from the Camry, so it had everything we wanted, plus some. It cost just a few thousand dollars more, but we were willing to spend it for the luxury we'd gain.

We talked with a car broker and asked him to find us an Avalon. He suggested that we consider a Lexus sedan instead, since they are more plentiful and priced just slightly more than the Avalon. He explained to Marco that Lexus is owned by Toyota, and our sedan would be built on a Toyota chassis, so it wasn't a radical departure from what we set out to get—just a slight upgrade.

He found us a beautiful two-tone gray Lexus ES 300 for $21,500. We financed 100 percent of it (and were giddy that the bank deemed us credit-worthy enough to offer us that kind of money with nothing down). We could have gotten a $15,000 Toyota Camry, but after seeing better cars in the Avalon and Lexus, we were no longer content with the idea of having a Camry. It had become a somewhat less-than option for us.

It's Consumerism

"I'll fake it 'til I make it" is an attitude of consumption. When this attitude is at work, you'll buy a good or service not only because that thing has intrinsic value to you, but because having it displays wealth. You may be attempting to display wealth to those around you and increase a perception of your social status. You may be trying to convince yourself that you have a level of wealth and, therefore, increase your personal sense of accomplishment.

It's like you've taken psychologist Abraham Maslow's hierarchy of needs and are trying to "buy up." Maslow ordered human needs (see diagram). He says that buying the thing you desire will indirectly meet some social need or need for esteem—which are higher levels, according to Maslow. Those needs are psychological and emotional, so a physical item can't meet the need. But the ownership of the good or service can change your perception of yourself or others' perception of you.

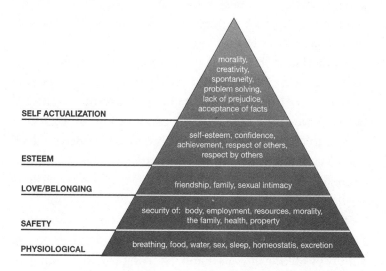

Consumerism is an epidemic worldwide. It is the act of consuming an increasing amount of things. Almost a decade ago, *National Geographic* estimated that the "consumer class" contains roughly 1.7 billion people worldwide. This consumer class is "the group of people characterized by diets of highly processed food, desire for bigger houses, more and bigger cars, higher levels of debt, and lifestyles devoted to the accumulation of non-essential goods."[1]

Sounds like us, doesn't it?

It's Called Marketing

As America is coming out of the greatest recession we've seen in a generation, we hear talk every day that touts consumerism as something positive. Economists want us to spend an increasing amount of money and borrow beyond that for things we can't truly afford. Consumer spending accounts for 70 percent of the economic activity in the United States;[2] our economy's growth is dependent on our increased consumption. That's scary to me.

Marketing is the vehicle used "to control and drive consumer behavior" toward the desired consumption.[3] The goal of marketers is to get products to appeal to our emotional needs. Advertising tries to connect ownership of a good or service to an increased social status or sense of personal accomplishment. It's intentional that marketers craft advertising campaigns and slogans that connect to Maslow's higher-level needs; they're taught to do so in their MBA programs.[4]

Take, for example, an Apple iPhone commercial called "Rock God." A young man creates a rock band in his garage simply by talking into his iPhone, starting with the comment, "I've got to get a guitar." Apple positions their product as a means to accomplish fame and popularity.

A commercial for the Mazda CX-5 crossover makes a direct appeal to our human need for significance. After showing lesser-than vehicles, the ad then shows researchers developing something that supersedes the competition. The commercial ends with the words "Better, stronger, smarter." Yes, those words reference the vehicle, but they are intentionally placed to help you think you'll be better, stronger, and smarter for buying what they are selling.

It isn't just advertisements that bombard us with consumerism messaging. Television shows and other forms of media do the same thing. For instance, the popular show *Celebrity Apprentice* opens with the theme song "For the Love of Money" by the O'Jays, where the word *money* is repeated

over twenty times in the first minute of the song. Not just
that, but Donald Trump, the central character on the show,
is an American icon of extravagant living. His second wife's
wedding ring cost $250,000, and the ring he bought his third
wife is reported to have cost $1 to $2 million.[5] Millions of
Americans watch each week to see who Donald Trump will
fire, reinforcing the idea that being rich and powerful go hand
in hand.

What I Thought Wealthy Was

"Honey, look," I said to Marco at a stoplight. "Look at that
car." I had noticed a Jaguar in the lane next to us, and since
luxury cars are rare around here, I pointed it out to him.

"Hmm . . . I wonder what they do for a living?" Marco
said. We bantered ideas about all sorts of high-income jobs.
The light turned green and Marco verbalized what I was also
thinking: "I don't know what they do, but you've got to be
rich to drive something like that."

While we embraced I'll-fake-it-'til-I-make-it thinking, we
judged wealth by what people bought and how much they
spent. To us, the wealthy earned high incomes. We would
never dream to ask someone how much they make, so instead
we'd guess their income based on their spending habits. If they
spent a lot, and spent it on top-notch things, then certainly
they had to be wealthy.

Our Desire for Wealth

We wanted to be wealthy. We never expected to grace the show
Lifestyles of the Rich and Famous, but we always wanted
to have more than enough. It even came up during Marco's

wedding proposal to me. He proposed on a hill overlooking a river bluff. He said the place was symbolic of our financial future, when we would be on top and not on the bottom (we were close to the bottom when we got engaged).

At one point we thought we'd started to understand money. I worked for a family of millionaires who owned a number of fast-food franchises, temporary staffing companies, and banks. They worked, played, traveled, and spent what, when, and however much they wanted. I observed their habits and tastes, and then we emulated them.

It was while I worked for them that we bought our Lexus. We justified our dissatisfaction with the lower-level Toyota Camry with twisted logic. We didn't want to settle for less than what we truly desired. We started regularly eating at very expensive steakhouses. One birthday dinner cost Marco and me $150, plus tip, and that was just food and dessert, since we don't drink alcohol.

We Tried to Fake It

I can see now that we were entrenched in I'll-fake-it-'til-I-make-it thinking. We wanted to impress those around us (although we would have denied it at the time). We figured that if we pulled up in a Lexus and talked about our night out at such-and-such fancy schmancy steakhouse, then friends and family would assume we had some level of wealth. In turn, they might think a little better about us and we'd think better of ourselves.

I'd heard "I'll fake it 'til I make it" referring to other things in life, and it made good sense to me. Think of a public speaking coach talking to a nervous student. The coach says, "Even if you don't feel confident, act confident. Trust me: You step on the stage exuding a self-created confidence, and the feel-ings of confidence will follow." The idea is that if you start acting in a certain way, even against your feelings, then like a self-fulfilling prophecy, the thing you desire will come to pass.

Deep down we hoped that acting like my rich boss would work for us, like the placebo effect works in patients who expect improvement in their health—they consistently see improvements, even when they are not given any new medicine or medical treatment.[6] We were buying things *in anticipation* of becoming wealthy, whereas my boss was wealthy *before* he made similar purchases.

We Misunderstood Wealth

I no longer measure wealth by the amount or types of things people consume. Drs. Thomas Stanley and William Danko set me straight in their book *The Millionaire Next Door* (Longstreet Press, 1996). Stanley and Danko are the nation's foremost experts about America's millionaires. When Marco and I understood that the wealthy aren't what the media portray but something entirely different, we felt empowered to walk away from consumerism. (I have to say that I also felt angry that I'd believed the façade of high consumption as an indication of wealth for many years, so consider yourself warned.)

Who Are America's Millionaires?

Only 4.9 percent of Americans are bona fide millionaires.[7] I better start by explaining what I mean when I use the descrip-tor *millionaire*. I'm not judging someone based on income. In fact, American millionaires' median taxable income is

$185,000.[8] It's just a small minority, less than 10 percent, who have an annual taxable income of more than a million dollars.[9]

I'm judging based on net worth. Net worth is a figure representing what you've accumulated over time (your assets) minus whatever debt or other financial liabilities you might have. Very few of us get to the place where our net worth is over a million bucks.

Where I focused on amassing personal belongings to look wealthy, in reality, personal belongings are a small portion of a millionaire's asset portfolio. Think about it. Most things we buy depreciate in value. Someone wise with her money won't see dishes, cars, clothes, and shoes as long-term assets. Instead, the affluent focus on building monetary savings and income-producing assets like businesses and bona fide investments. They've amassed, on average, about $2.2 million each.[10]

The Tightwads

You might imagine that most of the affluent inherited money, like the Kennedys. Surprisingly, 80 percent of America's millionaires are first-generation millionaires. That's good news for you and me, who come from non-millionaire families, because there's hope for us to achieve real wealth—not this pseudo-wealth-based-on-consumption stuff we've tried before.

They are mainly self-employed business owners in dull occupations. Their job titles include things like welder, auctioneer, exterminator, and plumbing contractor.[11] That explains why their incomes aren't huge—they're regular upper-middle-class folks.

Since their incomes aren't seven figures, there's only one way they've been able to build savings and assets in excess of a million dollars—frugality. Most American millionaires share a fundamental belief that it's important to live within your means.[12]

In fact, Stanley and Danko went so far as to call them tightwads.[13]

That, my friends, is music to my ears.

How the Rich Really Live

I have a retort now when I see a young man surrounded by luxury goods like fancy cars and big boats, then hear the commercial's announcer say, "Swipe your card and the world is yours. Live rich." I can talk right back to the television and say, "You're lying! That's not how the rich live and I won't believe you."

Yes, some wealthy folks are extravagant. Donald Trump, my former boss, and many others. But the majority of America's millionaires aren't. Listen to these surprising—actually shocking—facts about America's wealthiest households:

- 71 percent create a grocery shopping list before heading to the store.[14]
- 70 percent regularly have shoes resoled or repaired instead of buying new ones.[15]
- The majority have never paid more than $575 for a suit.[16]
- 48 percent of millionaires regularly reupholster furniture instead of buying new.[17]
- Only a minority drive current-model-year cars.[18]
- Only a minority have ever leased a car.[19]

- They typically spend $34,000 on a car, which is not that far off from the $29,000 that an average American pays.[20]
- Their homes are worth an average of $440,000.[21]
- Only 1 percent of them have *ever* paid more than $925 for a pair of shoes.[22]

Another distinction of this group includes their distaste for debt. Most have little or no debt, including only a small balance on their mortgage—if they carry a balance at all.[23]

Satisfaction Is the Antidote

Understanding the wealthy was powerful to Marco and me because it shattered so much of what we thought we were chasing after. When we realized that consumption is not a goal of the affluent, we felt empowered to lay it down as a goal of ours. We replaced I'll-fake-it-'til-I-make-it consumerism with an attitude of satisfaction.

Consumption is not a goal of the affluent.

We were like Guido, the Venetian rat in one of my kids' storybooks. Guido works as a gondola ferryman. One day a passenger tells him about a bigger boat and paints an idea of a better life. Guido considers it, then buys the bigger boat. He obtains a number of larger boats until he finally has an ocean-going vessel. He sets sail thinking he's reached the pinnacle of existence, but in a quiet moment realizes he misses everything he left behind. He thought bigger boats would provide deeper satisfaction, but he was wrong. One day he cries out, "Enough is enough!" He returns to Venice and swaps his huge ship for a small gondola. He lives out a contented life ferrying tourists.[24]

It Does Not Come Easy

Satisfaction sounds like a great plan, but it does not come naturally to me. Even with small things, I'm inclined to be dissatisfied. For instance, I have a sweet tooth, and York Peppermint Patties are among my favorite candies. I prefer them over the other brands of chocolate-covered mints. In college I got a bag of the candies for my birthday. Before I'd finished chewing the first one, I said, "Mmm . . . the next one will taste so good," and I unwrapped the foil on my next mint.

A wise friend heard me say that and challenged me. He said, "Carrie, you haven't even finished your first Peppermint Pattie and you are already talking about the next one you're going to eat. Stop. Enjoy the one you're eating. Then enjoy the next one."

I was not enjoying what I had because my eyes were focused on what I wanted. Financially, this kind of dissatisfaction can be very costly. I have friends who lived in a 1970s split-level house in the suburbs. From the day they moved into that house, they weren't happy with it. They felt like it was dated and too small. Even with new carpet and paint, they never loved the house.

He worked in construction and rubbed elbows with a developer who offered them a way to acquire a $1 million home on their $90,000 annual income. It seemed a dream opportunity for them to acquire what they had always wanted.

It turned into a nightmare when the housing bubble burst and mortgage regulations changed. They couldn't refinance from their construction loan into their final mortgage because of regulation changes. That was a fatal problem. They had planned to refinance for significantly more than what they owed the developer, take the difference out in cash, and invest it. We're talking $400,000 they'd hoped to invest so that they could use the interest and dividends to pay their house payment.

They lost their million-dollar house. They lost their original house. The ripple effect of their dissatisfaction-motivated decision to pursue a bigger house had decimated their finances.

How to Be Satisfied

I'm not perfect, but I have come a long way in my quest to be satisfied with what Marco and I have. The battle to be satisfied is a battle of focus. We often spend our time mulling over what we don't have instead of considering the benefits of what we already possess. To walk in a place of contentment, there are two things you have to do:

1. Focus on the good aspects of what you already have.
2. Stop thinking about what you don't have.

You might say that I'm advocating for the cliché "attitude of gratitude." Yes, but I'm not just saying "Go, be, and feel grateful." I'm telling you exactly what to do to generate a sense of satisfaction inside you for the things you already own.

Let's consider a real-life example. Years after we bought our Lexus, Marco and I were in the market for another vehicle. This time we wanted a minivan. We'd saved $18,000 to pay cash for it. Again, we were interested in Toyota models and used a broker who shopped for us. He led us to a slightly-better-than-base model Toyota Sienna van with non-heated, non-leather seats, only one power sliding door, one power front bucket seat, and no sunroof. It was the make, model, and year we wanted. It was clean with low mileage, but it was certainly not as comfortable as our Lexus sedan.

For about $3,000 more we could get a better model with more features. We considered it but approached the decision differently than we had with our last car. This time Marco asked me, "Do you know how much work we have to do to earn and save $3,000?" I did. "Are leather seats worth that?" Nope.

We skipped the better van this time, but on one condition. Marco and I agreed to never ever complain about what our van lacks compared to any other van we'd ever see. We wouldn't think about what we didn't have.

I'm not advocating that you walk around mindlessly saying "I'm thankful to have this jalopy of a car" while internally your attitude screams "I'll fake it 'til I make it!" Your unspoken self-talk is still considering everything that is wrong with your car. You aren't allowing yourself to consciously consider the things that are right with the car you have.

Your list of the positive aspects of your car might include things like these:

- It starts reliably, even in Minnesota winters.
- It is paid for.
- It enables you to get to work, and work supports your family.
- It has the only cassette-tape player you still own, which allows you to introduce your kids to the music you grew up listening to.

Your list of positive aspects might be short, but the length doesn't matter. It's your personal choice to focus on those positive things that does make a difference.

Stop Complaining

When Marco and I decided to buy our minivan with fewer features than we might have ideally liked, we chose to be grateful that we paid cash for it. We appreciate the layout of the interior space. We like the clean body. We like its low miles. Those are the things we think and talk about.

You're not superhuman, and neither am I. Complaints and grievances about your current possessions will still rise up in your thinking. But just because the thought enters your mind does not mean you need to let it dwell there. When you find yourself rehearsing a negative aspect of your current belongings, you have to choose to supplant that thought. You supplant it with thoughts and words about the thing's positive aspects.

It's that battle for your attention. I'm not talking about how you feel. I'm talking about consciously putting your attention on these positive aspects of the things you currently own.

The Phrase to Judge By

Focusing on the good in what you have is not enough to stop a drive for consumption. You also have to stop thinking about what you don't have. Wait a second, am I saying that you can't want or dream of a nicer car? Or a better house? No, I'm not. It's all about how you do it.

We discussed the critical importance of long-range dreams and goals in chapter 3, and we discussed short- and midterm goals in chapter 4. Thinking about your future and planning for future purchases is a good and healthy discipline. Yet I'm saying that to combat consumerism, you cannot focus your attention on what you don't have. Let me explain the seeming contradiction.

We are talking about satisfaction as the antidote for consumerism. There is a way you can determine whether every goal and dream is rooted in consumerism. If your thoughts about the item you want sound like, *I'll be happy when I get* . . . then you need to stop thinking about that thing you want.

In November 2008 Marco and I made our final payment on the nearly $60,000 we had in debt. The mortgage on our townhouse was our only outstanding debt. We had a toddler and another baby on the way. Our two-bedroom, 1,500-square-foot townhouse facing a busy road didn't seem like an ideal place for raising a family. We wanted a different house.

After having paid off our debt, we felt positioned to get a single-family home. The housing market had started its slide, so we planned to buy something different and rent our townhouse because we were upside down on the mortgage.

We found a nice five-bedroom house on a suburban cul-de-sac. We made an offer on it because it allowed us to escape everything we disliked about our current home. It had more space on a quiet street, but it also had a larger kitchen, a nicer deck, and more natural light. Marco and I had never articulated to one another how much the kitchen, deck, and lighting in our townhouse bothered us, but those things came up when we saw this house.

We were more convinced than ever that our townhouse was not a good long-term fit for us. When the owners accepted our offer on the five-bedroom home, we knew we'd be happier when we could move in. The deal fell through, though, and we never did buy that house.

Spending Follows Contentment

That experience jolted something inside Marco and me. We realized that even though we'd paid off our debt, the consumerism attitude had not died in us. We were inches from making a significant financial decision that was motivated by discontent.

We repented of that to one another. We decided that we would be content in our townhouse if we lived there forever. Our conversation shifted from everything we didn't like about our home to the things we did like. Instead of figuring out a plan to escape what we had, we talked about how to make it work.

One day in the summer of 2011, I sat outside on our little patio watching my kids ride bikes on the sidewalk. Four lanes of traffic traveled the road just behind a tree-lined barrier thirty feet from us. And I thought, *I love it here.* I appreciated the long, flat sidewalk for bike riding. I'd tell Marco, "Many people's driveways are too steep for kids to ride bikes safely. We are really blessed to have this."

Marco loved it too. He and our girls would use binoculars to look at the birds and squirrels in the trees on our association's property. He'd comment about how so many new homes don't have mature trees like ours and what a great teaching opportunity it created for him and our kids.

We were content. We didn't need another house, a bigger house, a newer house, a better yard, or a quieter street to bring happiness. We were happy with what we had. We weren't looking for anything else.

After our hearts had completely settled on the fact that we'd be happy in our townhouse until the girls graduated from high school, something interesting happened. We felt a divine nudge on the inside to move. This time, however, our motivation was fiscal responsibility. The housing market was changing and we ran numbers that confirmed the financial sense of buying a single-family home now, while the market was still depressed, and selling our townhouse. It fit with our long-term investment strategy.

We moved in January 2012. We were like kids on Christmas morning the first few days in our new house. Marco and I would exclaim to one another, "Wow! Did you see this?" and "Whoa! This part of the house is so cool." We had become so content with what we had that we'd actually forgotten about the annoyances of our townhouse.

For instance, our old house was four levels, which means a lot, a lot of stairs. Our new house is a rambler. I had come to appreciate the stairs in our townhouse both as a means for exercise (I'd run up and down them for fitness) and as a way to break up our living spaces. It wasn't until the first time I vacuumed, and only had a dozen stairs to do, that I realized I was glad to not have as many. Not once in our buying process did I think, *I can't wait to get into this new house so I won't have so many stairs to contend with.*

Turn Off and Tune Out Advertising

Friends, we do live in a society that pushes consumption as something glamorous. Those messages are powerful and are coming at us a thousand times a day on TV, on the radio, and in magazines. If you're serious about being satisfied with what you have instead of dissatisfied with what you don't, then you need to turn off and tune out the advertising.

Advertising is effective at getting you to want things you didn't know you needed. At my house we avoid advertising when we can—we listen to commercial-free radio. We turn it off when advertising is unavoidable—we mute television commercials and skip the temptation to thumb through the Sunday paper's sales flyers. We consciously ignore it when it can't be avoided—like the ads in magazines.

I want my purchases to spring from an intrinsic desire. I am able to discern what I want for myself. My husband and I can establish our desires for our family. We do not need the influence of marketers—with their selfish agenda to sell us products and services—to influence our buying behavior.

Quiz

Are you trying to impress either yourself or others with your purchases? Here's a quiz that may help reveal your own internal attitudes. Using the following chart, place a number after every statement.

1 = Never	2 = Rarely	3 = Sometimes	4 = Frequently	5 = Always

1. I believe my housing and clothes should say something about my level of success.
2. I often find myself judging others by the cars they drive, houses they live in, or toys they own.
3. When someone I know acquires something that is nicer than what I have, I often feel a tinge of jealousy.
4. My purchases are often inspired by what I see and hear in the media, whether TV shows, advertising, magazines, blogs, or radio.

Tally your scores. Your total demonstrates how strongly you hold the attitude that what people own determines their value in society.

0–6: This attitude has minimal influence on your financial decision making. Other attitudes may need addressing first.

7–13: This attitude is part of your financial decision-making process. For your long-term success it needs to be addressed.

14–20: This attitude strongly influences your financial decisions. It is a priority to change this attitude.

Discussion Questions

Here are a few questions to help you think through your own financial situation, by yourself or with a small group:

1. Make a list of what you love about your current house. What are some of the advantages you have now that you wouldn't have if your house were bigger or newer or in a different neighborhood?

2. How did the discussion of millionaires' lifestyles impact you? What can you do to live more like the millionaire next door?

3. What are some ways to avoid the lure of advertising? Are there particular television shows or magazines that lead to the desire for more luxuries in your life? What can you do to protect yourself from these enticements?

4. What are some creative ways you can satisfy your desire for the "finer things" without spending much money?

6

I can't afford it

That's what I consider true generosity: You give your all and yet you always feel as if it costs you nothing.

Simone de Beauvoir

*M*arco was bursting with excitement when he got home from his first international business trip. He loved Mexico, from the historical sites he saw to the business contacts he made. As he unpacked his suitcase, I could tell what was really behind my generous, gift-giving husband's exuberance. He spent part of a day in a Mexican market and came home with a suitcase full of gifts for me and other family members.

As he pulled each one out, he explained what he was thinking when he bought it, and how he thought each gift would be a good fit for the recipient. He bought me a traditional Mexican doll, a wooden serving platter, painted hollowed gourds that could be used as candy dishes, and a sterling silver necklace with matching earrings.

"I have one more thing," Marco said, beaming from ear to ear. "I *really* think you're going to like this." Then he took a beautiful hip-length black leather coat out of his suitcase. I could tell just by looking at it that it was an expensive, well-made coat. "This is for you. I thought you'd look nice in it. I noticed you didn't have a fall coat to wear with your business suits."

"You bought that? In Mexico? For me?" I was uncomfortable with the thought of these lavish gifts. *They're too much. We can't afford them. I'd never buy that expensive of a coat,* I told myself.

Marco must have read my mind, because he said, "Don't worry about the money, Carrie. All of this is paid for with the overtime I worked while I was there. Even the coat."

Marco's overtime earnings were always his to spend as he desired. What an incredibly thoughtful and generous thing he had done in choosing to give them up for me. Yet I couldn't help feeling uneasy. I knew we could afford it; I just tend to have a can't-afford-it attitude.

I Can't Afford It

The I-can't-afford-it attitude harbors guilt or shame when spending money. Addressing this underlying shame is important to relieving lifetime financial stress. In my situation with Marco, I felt guilty receiving such generous gifts. I felt like the money should be used on other things—not on me. If I take an honest look deeper down within me, I actually felt like I didn't deserve all these gifts. I hadn't done anything to merit them. It wasn't my birthday. It wasn't Christmas. So instead of receiving his loving gesture, I bristled at it.

This attitude takes admirable traits to excess. It's like an antique collector turned hoarder. Collecting is a fine hobby. You derive pleasure from it. You enjoy it with loved ones. It has an appropriate, peripheral place in your life. Hoarding is that behavior in the extreme. You collect so much of everything that it becomes difficult to maneuver in your home. It becomes embarrassing to have people over. It divides you from those you love. It takes a front seat in your life, impacting many other behaviors and choices in detrimental ways.

What starts out as a healthy self-control in spending becomes deprivation. It is good and right to live within your means and tell yourself, "No, I won't spend money on that now; we have more pressing priorities." It's not a good thing for you to buy cheap shoes that hurt your feet when you could afford others, simply because the thought of spending sixty dollars on a pair of shoes makes you uneasy.

The I-can't-afford-it attitude takes an ability to delay gratification and turns it into a refusal to ever be gratified. You see a piece of workout equipment that you'd like to have and know you'd enjoy. It's okay to say, "I'll save my money and come back in six months to buy this with cash." "I can't afford it" feels like it's not okay to set aside money for yourself, even if it is in moderation and for something you'd enjoy, when your family has other needs.

Identifying where healthy financial management traits, like frugality, turn detrimental is subjective and varied from person to person. I believe there are two tests you use in any situation to decide whether you are exercising a healthy restraint or feeding an I-can't-afford-it attitude.

The Happy Test

I want to help you discern which behaviors are healthy and frugal and which ones are motivated from this I-can't-afford-it attitude. It's not as simple as saying that buying off-brand cereal in bags versus the name-brand boxed cereal equals an I-can't-afford-it attitude. Most behavior is moderate enough that a surface judgment is not sufficient. You need to look underneath the behavior to the emotions behind the decision.

Does your behavior make you happy? That is the first litmus test of this attitude. Remember that an I-can't-afford-it attitude carries shame or guilt when spending money. That's very different from making a choice that leads to happiness.

I think this is best explained with a couple of examples where I've discerned my own boundary between frugal and "I can't afford it."

Zip-top bags

For years I've washed and reused zip-top bags until they get punctured and are no longer airtight. I think it is an easy way to extend the life of a disposable product, which saves me money in the long run. When we decided to live within our means, I looked for other possible ways to reduce our expenses.

I started thinking about all the items we throw away. If I reuse zip-top bags to save money, then maybe there are other things I can salvage from the trash to save a few bucks. The quest was on. I started using the plastic mesh bag you get when you buy onions or oranges as a replacement for a scour pad in the kitchen sink. I set aside egg cartons to use for sorting my daughter's hair binders by color. I'd use plastic containers from a pound of strawberries with a homemade bubble mixture to blow bubbles with my daughter in the springtime.

All those ideas are fine and good, but over time they started to mentally wear me out. I felt guilty every time I put something in the trash or recycling bin because I couldn't repurpose it somehow. I'd think, *I know I should wash this plastic bag from inside a cereal box so I can use it as a waxed paper, but I don't want to.* The things I was doing to pinch pennies were a drudgery to me. Washing plastic zip-top baggies was a fine frugal habit, but forcing myself to repurpose all my trash was an I-can't-afford-it attitude.

The dentist

I don't mind going to the dentist. Some people are phobic of the chair, the bright light, the whirl of the brush or drill, but not me. I've been known to fall asleep in the dentist's chair, so you know I find it relaxing. I also believe in the value of preventative care. Whether my car, my teeth, or my physical body, I want to stave off major trouble by providing routine care.

Marco is really solid on his routine cleanings and goes every six months. One time he came home, relaying the dentist's concern that I hadn't been to see him in over a year. I knew that and was hoping the topic wouldn't come up. I had been having a minor toothache and suspected that my next visit would include a recommendation for a crown—a $400 to $500 bill even after insurance. I didn't want to spend the money, so I was avoiding the dentist.

As soon as Marco and I started to talk about it, I felt embarrassed. I explained this as a self-sacrificing act for our family's greater good. I thought it was admirable that I'd extend my frugality this way. Marco disagreed. I finally acquiesced.

I really didn't feel happy about avoiding the dentist. If you had asked me, "Does this behavior make you happy?" I might have said yes. It made me happy to the extent that I would have felt *more* guilty for going to the dentist than I did for neglecting proper dental care. In a lesser-of-two-evils sort of way, yes, it made me happy. Well, pseudo-happy, in a martyr sort of way.

Meet the misers

My self-sacrificing attitude with the dentist is not much different from Richard Walters' attitude. When Walters died in 2007, he left a $4 million estate. He didn't have any children, had never married, and was estranged from his family. With no natural heirs, he left $400,000 each for National Public Radio; the Catholic Mission of Mercy in Phoenix, Arizona; and several other nonprofits. He also left an undisclosed amount for Rita Belle, a registered nurse he drank coffee with at a local senior center.

Walters was a distinguished man. During the Korean War he served in the marines. He graduated with honors from Purdue University, holding a degree in mechanical engineering. Later he obtained a master's degree in teaching from Ball State University. He worked in the aerospace industry for twenty-three years, then was forced into an early retirement.

Yet Walters was different from almost any other man who has died with a seven-figure estate. Richard Walters was homeless. He slept on the grounds of the senior center where he and Belle drank coffee. He ate at an area hospital and used the hospital's telephone when he needed to make a call.[1]

You could call both Richard Walters and me misers. The word *miser* shares a root with the word *miserable*, and rightfully so.[2] Misers refuse to spend money to the point that they make themselves miserable in one way or another. Their behavior doesn't pass our happy test.

The Relationship Test

Other people's money decisions impact you; your money decisions impact other people. The second test to help you discern whether a behavior is grounded in a healthy frugality or comes from I-can't-afford-it thinking is the relationship test. Are your loved ones or relationships being hindered or damaged, directly or indirectly as a result of your choice? Appropriate frugal choices work for both you and your loved ones.

Frugal rules

You probably have at least a few things you do to stretch a buck. You unplug your coffeepot after you pour the last cup because you don't want it to siphon off extra electricity. You limit yourself to four squares of toilet paper every time you go because it makes a roll last so much longer. You don't turn on the air-conditioning until it's ninety-five degrees outside. Fine.

But you may be in a family where your husband forgets to unplug the coffeepot; your school-aged children and their friends are frivolous with toilet paper and use an entire roll in an afternoon; your teenage daughter turns on the air when it's eighty-five degrees because it's too warm for her to sleep.

When you live in a community or family, then your frugal rules can't pass just your happiness test. They need to be accepted by those around you. It's not right for your rules to make people in your life miserable. Their misery may come because they need more than four squares of toilet paper and feel perpetually guilty for doing so. Or it may come from your scolding them for not living up to your standard.

I hear a lot about this when I teach classes about saving money on groceries. Attendees have often made a personal rule that they won't buy anything unless it is on sale and they also have a coupon. That's a fine way to live, except when it's not.

One summer my friend's husband asked his wife to pick up his favorite brand of steak sauce next time she went to the store because they'd run out. As Amy stood in the steak sauce aisle, she felt torn. A bottle of steak sauce cost almost $3.50. She was certain she'd seen it on sale a few weeks back and knew that if she waited another week or two, she might get it for $1.50.

It's important to let people influence the money decisions that impact them. Amy did that by choosing to buy the steak sauce. She valued her husband above her rule by telling herself, "The steak sauce is not worth $3.50, but my husband is."

Conflict avoidance

"I can't afford it" can also be a phrase used to avoid interpersonal conflict. Imagine you are in a superstore with your child. You pass through the toy section on your way to the checkout lanes when your son spots something he really wants. He picks it up, admires the box, then looks at you with puppy-dog eyes and asks, "Can I have it?"

You reply, "No, honey, we can't afford it." The truth is, you probably *could* afford it. Your shopping cart might contain forty dollars in nonessential items that you could swap out for the toy. If money was tight, I bet you'd find a way to get him a toy if his birthday was tomorrow.

What you probably meant to say was something like, "No, I am not going to buy that for you right now" or "No, we have other things we are spending our money on today." But in telling him that you can't afford it, you have planted a seed in his mind about your ability to provide for him. Then when the time comes that you do buy him a toy, he'll wonder where the money came from.

I know how this works in kids because I was one. I remember being a senior in high school and pleading with my mom to buy my graduation pictures. I'd had the sitting, but we had to buy several hundred dollars' worth to get the developed portraits back. Her response was always "We can't afford it."

Then, on the evening of my golden birthday, I found a surprise on my bed. My mom had gotten the portraits. I was excited. I had wanted them. But I also felt tremendously guilty. I had heard her say we couldn't afford them, but here they were. It felt wrong for me to have them. There were probably better things my mom could have spent the money on.

Be aware that what you say does register with your kids, so be sure to tell them what you really mean. Use phrases that provide them assurance of provision instead of creating a fear of lack. "I'm working on it, Carrie. We'll get them just as soon as I can," or "You are going to have to wait, but we will eventually get them. Just not today," may have been better phrases for my mom to use.

Greed: The Ugly Truth

Greed is the driving force behind this attitude. It is nothing more than an excessive desire to accumulate money.[3] This is different from the desire to flaunt money, which we saw in "I'll Fake It 'Til I Make It."

Ebenezer Scrooge from Charles Dickens's *A Christmas Carol* is the personification of greed. Scrooge is a successful business owner, but he is thoroughly unhappy with himself and those around him. He despises the poor. He hoards his money. He treats his employee, Bob Cratchit, terribly. If you dig even deeper, you can see a desire for control and fear of the future as impetuses for greed.

Control issues

Greed can be a grasping for control. For me, I get queasy in my stomach at the thought of being out of control, without a plan to regain traction. I can Band-Aid that discomfort by finding something, anything, to control. Finances are an easy target.

Michelangelo, the famous artist who painted the ceiling in the Sistine Chapel, is like me in that way. He was a control freak on the projects he took on,[4] and he was as miserly as they come. As the story goes, he bragged to an apprentice that "however rich I may have been, I have always lived like a poor man."[5] His drive to work and earn was so strong that he frequently slept with his boots on so he wouldn't waste a minute on everyday essentials such as dressing and undressing. When he finally did take them off, the skin of his foot came off as well (ew, that's gross).[6] This control-based greed comes from a man worth more than $700 million dollars by today's standards.[7]

This kind of grasping for control via hyper-restraint is similar to what an anorexic experiences. She is excessively restrictive of her calories in an attempt to feel control over life. But that control is a mirage. It's better to acknowledge your powerlessness to influence many of life's events. As Alcoholics Anonymous would say, turn to a Higher Power.

I have made strides in overcoming my I-can't-afford-it attitude by being aware that there is a mighty God running the universe, and He doesn't need me to copilot.

Self-esteem needs

Greed can also stem from a desire to boost your own self-esteem. Self-esteem is your self-acceptance stemming from your own appraisal of your worth, significance, attractiveness, competence, and ability to satisfy your aspirations.[8] At times you may not see your own value.

In those moments you may turn to unhealthy behaviors that create a false sense of worth. Greed is one of those. You see yourself as having a superior level of self-control. Others are too weak to resist the temptations that you can easily ignore. And it makes you feel better about yourself.

This mind-set is dangerous because it perpetuates the unhealthy I-can't-afford-it attitude. You've convinced yourself that an unhealthy trait you possess (hyper-restriction and greed) is good, even enviable. A hoarder does something similar by convincing herself that each item in her home is unique. A hoarder can't see that yellow yarn, pale yellow yarn, saffron yellow yarn, and sunflower yellow yarn could all get grouped together as "yellow yarn." Since each skein of yarn is unique, each one is more valuable than the last. So valuable, in fact, that she can't part with any of them.[9]

Fear of an uncertain future

Spending and saving decisions are often predicated on our confidence level about the future. When you feel like tomorrow is a solid, sure thing, then you are more apt to freely spend today. When tomorrow feels uncertain, then you'd prefer to save your money "just in case." These are typical influencers of our financial habits.

When fear of the future becomes strong, it can create a desire to hoard. Think of what our parents or grandparents went through in the Great Depression. It was a time when millions of people worldwide felt like the bottom fell out from under them. It was an era when fifty Chicagoans were reported to have fought over a barrel of garbage because it represented food scraps for their families.[10] It was a time when 2.25 million children left school to work in factories in hopes of supporting their families.[11]

I think of my grandmother, who grew up in those desperate, poor times. She freezes packs of chewing gum so they last longer. She refrigerates most everything—including cooking oil and shelf-stable items—because she's afraid of premature spoiling. Leaving the door open too long in the summertime will be met with one of her hollers: "In or out! We aren't paying to air-condition the yard!"

I see these same things in me after my family's dramatic change from upper middle class to lower middle class in one month's time. I often wonder when the rug of financial stability will be pulled out from underneath me. As a result, I desire to conserve what I have today.

Now or never

Conversely, while for many of us, fear of the future causes a hoarding-like mentality, others may find themselves frantically buying things they've been wanting when a little extra money comes along. For instance, let's imagine that you are working hard to pay off your debt. One of the things you have cut out of your spending plan is getting your hair professionally colored. You've gotten pretty good at doing it yourself, but your niece is getting married next week and you keep thinking about how you would really like to look your best for the family photo. You go to the mailbox and find a check for seventy-five dollars from a friend you loaned money to months ago. Excited, you run inside and call your stylist to make an appointment. While making that appointment may not reveal a fear of the future for some of us, if you examine your motive, you might find a hidden fear that if you didn't take this opportunity for yourself, you would never have the luxury of a salon visit again.

Now let's imagine you back at the mailbox. You see the check and immediately envision those caramel highlights, but rather than running to your phone, you stop and remind yourself of your big-picture goals. You choose to see that seventy-dollar check as a snowflake in your snowball of debt payoff, which we'll discuss more in chapter 11. Sure, you could make that appointment, but you'd rather take a step toward creating a secure and debt-free future. You look forward to the day when you'll incorporate guilt-free salon visits back into your spending plan.

The Antidote: Become Generous

Students at the University of British Columbia played a game in blind pairs (where their partner's identity was concealed from them). One partner received ten one-dollar coins as a reward for participating in the game. The other partner received no compensation.

The student who possessed the ten dollars was given the option to donate a portion of their money to the other student, whose identity had yet to be revealed. Each student had one stipulation: The giver had to hand-deliver whatever amount he or she decided to give, zero to ten dollars. The receiving student could not dispute the amount, even if it was nothing. The generous students were compared against the stingy ones. The study found that the generous ones were happier; the stingy ones felt more shame. Researchers examined the results and concluded, "Stingy economic behavior can produce a feeling of shame."[12]

The antidote to the I-can't-afford-it feeling is generosity. Start with a commitment to give to others. You can derive *more* personal satisfaction from giving than you can from flexing your willpower muscle and restraining an expense.[13]

There are thousands of organizations doing incredible work around the world. Find one that matches your interests at CharityNavigator.org. Marco and I do the bulk of our giving through our local church. When we give there, we know we're supporting our pastor and staff, but we also know that some portion is being passed along to other groups in our city, nation, and around the world. Our giving helps me temper the I-can't-afford-it feeling of guilt or shame.

I tease my dad about a birthday dinner he bought me during my college years. He called in advance and said I could pick anywhere I wanted to eat. I was grateful for his generosity and eager to escape cafeteria food. I had a favorite place in mind. He arrived at my apartment, then fanned out a set of coupons and restated, "You can pick anywhere you want to eat," this time implying that I could choose anywhere he had a coupon for. His attempt at generosity was thwarted by his commitment to frugal rules—namely, you eat out only with a coupon. One baby step at a time, he's gotten more generous over the years, to the point that he contributed significantly to my wedding. That time there were no strings and no frugal rules attached. On my wedding day, my dad was filled with joy to see how happy his generous, no-strings-attached gift had made me and my new husband.

Don't forget yourself

When I think of generosity and giving, my mind rushes to think of those less fortunate than I am. Like I've said, that's a great place to start with your generosity, but don't end there.

If you battle this I-can't-afford-it mind-set, then you need to consciously make the effort to be generous to yourself as well. Set aside some fun money for yourself each month. Spend it on something you enjoy. While you spend it, refuse to feel guilty. Enjoy being good to yourself. If you can identify with the story about wanting to get your hair done, then diffuse the guilty feeling by setting aside twenty dollars each month. In a few months you can go get those highlights, go to that concert, or do something else you love and *can* afford.

This is something I need to put conscious effort toward or I'll fall back into I-can't-afford-it thinking. Most recently, I decided I want to buy a treadmill. It's a very big-ticket item for me, but it's something I've wanted for almost ten years.

It wasn't physically possible until recently, because our house was too small. Once we got into the larger space I waffled on my desire. I started to talk myself out of it. I fell into every I-can't-afford-it thought pattern and was almost ready to cross it off my wish list. But then I came to my senses and realized what I was doing.

I will get a treadmill (we're still saving our money). It will stand as a reminder for me that I can afford the things that are important to me.

Quiz

Do you often tell yourself "I can't afford it"? Here's a quiz that may help reveal your own internal attitudes. Using the following chart, place a number after every statement.

1 = Never	2 = Rarely	3 = Sometimes	4 = Frequently	5 = Always

1. I believe our income won't ever let us have certain niceties.
2. I often feel guilty about spending money on myself, even after I've carefully saved up for something.
3. I pride myself in setting certain "frugal" rules, such as never paying more than a certain price for a given food item or never eating in a restaurant without a coupon.
4. Having an ever-increasing savings account helps me feel greater control over my future.
5. Giving gifts to loved ones or to charitable organizations is difficult for me, even if I've financially prepared ahead of time.

Tally your scores. Your total demonstrates how strongly you hold the attitude that you "can't afford it."

0–8: This attitude has minimal influence on your financial decision making. Other attitudes may need addressing first.

9–17: This attitude is part of your financial decision-making process. For your long-term success it needs to be addressed.

18–25: This attitude strongly influences your financial decisions. It is a priority to change this attitude.

Discussion Questions

Here are a few questions to help you think through your own financial situation, by yourself or with a small group:

1. How do you feel when you receive gifts from your immediate family? Guilty? Grateful? What do you think that says about your I-can't-afford-it mentality?

2. What was your experience growing up in terms of what your family could or could not afford? How was this communicated to you by your parents?

3. Can you think of a time when one of your financial "rules" has made you less generous than you'd like to be?

4. Where in your life can you see evidence of greed? Keep in mind that this is something we all struggle with, just in different ways.

skills you need
to change your attitudes

*A*s I'm sure you know, wanting to change an attitude is very different from actually doing it. We've all experienced any number of things we'd like to change about ourselves, but when the rubber meets the road, we haven't managed to figure out how to make real change happen. Now is the time to move from theory to practice.

In this section we'll move away from talking about the attitudes themselves in order to discuss general strategies for revamping your thought life. Chapter 7 will look at certain "best practices" you can develop to move from destructive thought patterns to constructive ones. Chapter 8 will show you how to stand up to everyday pressures that will tempt you into your old ways of thinking. Then chapter 9 will give advice on how to make your changes stick over the long haul.

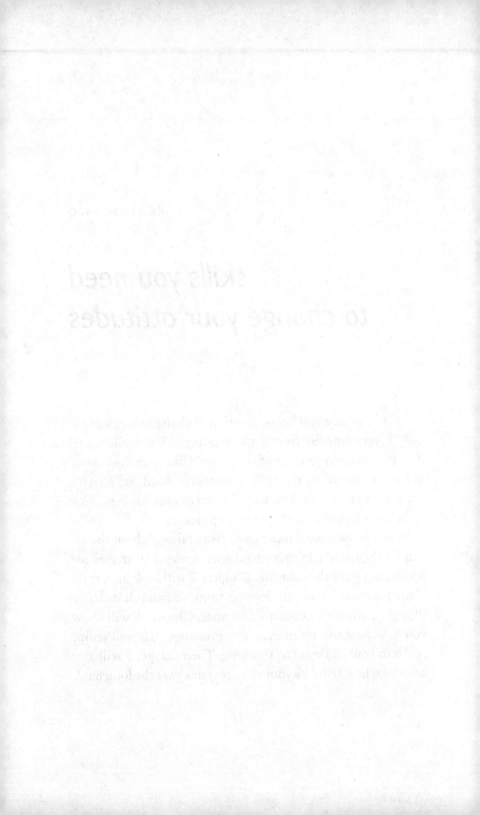

7

changing your self-talk

Say unto yourself what you'd have others say unto you.

—A twist on the Golden Rule

One morning during my sophomore year of high school, my classmates and I were settling into our desks. We were waiting for our humanities class to start. Mr. Olson, one of our teachers (we had two for that class), was interacting with a student from another one of his classes while my friends and I visited with one another.

A few minutes later the bell rang. The young man was still at Mr. Olson's desk, but it sounded like they were disagreeing about something. They raised their voices, stood up, and started to shove one another. The student knocked Mr. Olson to the ground, then took off running. Mr. Olson shouted a racial slur at the student, then stood up and took off running after him while we all watched wide-eyed with jaws dropped.

Moments later the classroom's phone rang. Mrs. Hein, our other humanities teacher, answered it. It was the office giving her instructions about how to proceed. Each student had to write out what we'd witnessed as an aid to the school's administration in their investigation.

Just as she collected our eyewitness accounts, Mr. Olson and the student both returned to the classroom. The two of them and Mrs. Hein proceeded to tell us that the entire event we'd just witnessed was staged—racial slur and all. It was the first lesson in a new unit about paradigms. It was also the first time in my life I thought about what I think about.

We spent that day, and many others, learning from "the event," as we called it. Each student read their eyewitness account out loud to the rest of us. No two accounts were identical. Each student thought differently about what had happened. There were issues of authority at play (teacher and student), race (the teacher was white and the student wasn't), and violence (shouting and pushing). Each of us interpreted these dynamics of the event based on our own background and life experiences. Interestingly, we were able to ascertain our own attitudes toward those various dynamics by examining the thoughts we had as the event unfolded. In essence, our thoughts were simply a manifestation of the paradigms, mind-set, or attitudes we brought into the situation.

Becoming Aware of Thought Patterns

Marco and I related to money based on attitudes that have roots from our childhoods. We were the proverbial old dogs who wanted to learn new tricks. But no matter how entrenched an attitude is in your life, it can be changed. What you need to know is that the primary battleground of where you'll fight for change is in your mind.

I believe that if you can discipline your mind to think correctly about money, then the discipline you need in your wallet will happen. That's true because change happens first on the inside, then shows up on the outside. Numerous times Marco has joined a health club with the idea that having a membership will motivate him to go work out. It has never happened that way. One time, though, he started to work out regularly on his own, and then he decided to join the health club. That is the only time he routinely went and made use of his membership. External factors don't change our internal nature. It's the other way around.

Changing your mind isn't as simple as deleting a song you don't like from your mp3 player and downloading a new one from the Internet. The process is not complicated, but it does take diligent effort. These are the three things you need to do to replace an old attitude with a new one.

1. **Decide to believe something new.** You have to make a deliberate choice about your new belief.
2. **Identify the old thought (the one you no longer want).** Listen to your self-talk to spot the thought pattern you have but want to change. Think about what may have caused these thoughts.
3. **Replace that old thought with a new one.** Consciously turn your thoughts to a new thought that is consistent with your new belief.

All day long your mind is filled with a running stream of self-talk. You talk to yourself about the events you experience: you notice someone's outfit; you wonder what your client thinks of you while you make a sales presentation. You talk to yourself about you: you grimace as you see yourself in the mirror when you step out of the shower; you doubt your ability to cook when you make a new recipe for dinner. You talk to yourself about a thousand other things as well.

Become a detective of your own mind. Slow yourself down long enough to hear that internal conversation in your mind and take note of it, especially concerning money and material possessions. It's been playing in your mind for so many years that you may not be fully aware of all that is going into your decision-making process.

As you try to identify your current old-thought patterns, you may find it helpful to keep a log of your thoughts for a while. As you do various money-related things like get paid, watch commercials, run to the store, read fashion magazines, look at bank balances, pay bills, or window-shop, keep notes about how you thought *and* felt before, during, and after the activity.

You may identify a trigger that sets off a particular thought pattern or notice a result that always comes after you feel a certain way. They may not be blatant thoughts like, *I am going to blow my entire paycheck at the casino.* We're too smart to tell ourselves something that obviously detrimental. We may guise and justify with the kinds of attitude statements we decided in section one, something like "I deserve a break. It's Friday. No harm going to the casino."

I can be a master of tricking myself with red-herring thoughts. I remember a hike I took during a summer that I spent at a ranch in the Rocky Mountains of Colorado. Mountain air is thinner than midwestern air, and I was out of breath after about six feet. I was afraid I wouldn't have the stamina to make it to the mountain peak my friends pointed to as our destination. I complained almost the entire way. My pack was too heavy. My shoes were too tight. This was

126

wrong; that was wrong. In all honesty, those things weren't really a problem. I was so afraid of failing to reach the peak that I planted excuses with every step so I could point to one of those if I fell short of my expectation.

For me on that mountainside, a journal of my thoughts and feelings might have helped me connect the fear I had of being outperformed by my athletic friends with the barrage of negative thoughts in my mind.

Whether you use a journal or are able to tune in to your thoughts without one, take time to write down some of the money-related thoughts and feelings you have. Look at the feelings you notice and try to back up a step and identify the thought that came just before the emotion. For me, at that ranch in Colorado, I thought, *I may not be able to climb that mountain,* and then felt anxious at the thought of doing it with my peers. If you feel anxious when you sit down to pay the bills, stop and identify the thought that came seconds before that. Was it *I wish we had more money?* or *I wonder what John overspent on this week?* or *If my parents knew about my situation, they'd be embarrassed of me?*

It is important that you allow yourself to experience that negative thought without suppressing it. You may think that I am asking you to push it away and pretend it doesn't exist. I'm not. I can't think of a single time in life when ignoring a problem made it go away. Healthy resolution to issues doesn't work that way. It's got to get aired out.

Replacement Thoughts

At bedtime my five-year-old daughter often complains about being afraid of monsters. We've tried every strategy under the sun to ease her fears. We've made "monster spray" that

127

we spray in her room to chase them away. We've played red light, green light, and the monsters always get a red light. We have prayed. We have opened closets and looked under the bed. We've left lights on and doors open. Each of those strategies has had only marginal success.

A few weeks back she brought home a coloring sheet from her Sunday school class that has eased monster fears for good. Their lesson that day was about thoughts. As Victoria explained it to me, and I confirmed it by reading the lesson notes on the backside of her coloring sheet, she had been having "junk thoughts" about monsters. "They are like garbage in my brain, Mom, except they don't stink the same way garbage does."

Her teachers gave her the example that junk thoughts are like birds: A bird might fly over her head just like a thought might enter her brain. Victoria realized that she had been allowing these junk thoughts to stay in her brain at bedtime, as if someone would let a bird build a nest in her hair. "I don't want a bird in my hair!" she declared.

"Mom, from now on at bedtime, you help me to think about good things, okay?" I agreed, and now our bedtime routine involves brainstorming a handful of healthy thoughts that she can use to replace the junk ones about monsters.

The only effective way to stop a thought is to supplant it with another thought. If I tell you not to think about a gray elephant, what are you thinking about? A gray elephant. Our minds don't turn off thoughts just because we say "Stop thinking about that." Like a naughty two-year-old who needs to be redirected to play politely, we have to redirect our minds to something else entirely.

Think of it like a ketchup bottle you've just used up. You want to clean it out so you can toss it into the recycling bin, but if you had to scoop and scrape out every last bit of ketchup with a spatula and spoon, it would take you all day, and there'd still be ketchup left. It would be so difficult to clean every crevice of the bottle. What if, instead of trying to extract the unwanted ketchup, you left it there and just filled the bottle with a stream of running water? After a few minutes of the water filling and overflowing from the bottle, guess what? It's clean. Really clean. When you put in enough clean water with sufficient force, the ketchup comes out without any effort.

That's how our minds work too. You need to put your energy toward finding positive phrases. Then when you hear yourself thinking old unwanted thoughts, you fill your mind with the new thoughts. They'll wash the old ones away.

As Marco and I got out of debt, we had a few phrases that were very meaningful to us. These were phrases we consistently used to replace the old thoughts that bombarded our minds. Take time to identify phrases that work for you. Here are a few of our new thoughts:

- We work too hard for our money to let it leak out of our life.
- It's not how much we make, but how much we keep that makes a difference.
- I'm grateful for what I have.
- We can afford anything we prioritize.

You may find that just a single phrase is what you need to say. The phrase can work like a motivational self-cue that helps you press through and keep going. For me, when dealing with life's stress around home, I often say out loud to myself, "You've got this." I'll repeat it a few times in increasing tones of confidence until I can face the situation before me. You may have a money phrase that works the same way for you. If not, find one!

Words Matter

A classic example of the power of replacement thoughts is the children's story *The Little Engine That Could*. If you remember, a train full of toys breaks down on the tracks and needs help getting to the other side of the mountain. A shiny new engine pulls up and hears the little train's plight, but won't pull it. A passenger engine, a freight engine, and a rusty old engine also refuse to help. Finally, a very small engine pulls up. He fears he isn't strong enough to do the job, but he wants to help. He chooses an unlikely belief—that he is indeed able to pull the other train—and gets to work. His efforts pay off as he pulls the other train up over the mountain. He becomes a famous train because for the entire way he declares that he thinks he can do it, and that confidence enables a great feat.

That little train did just what we are talking about. He chose a new attitude. He identified his negative thought (that he was too little), then replaced that thought by saying that he thought he could. We learn from him that words are powerful thought supplanters.

I'll prove it to you. In just a second I'm going to ask you to do a simple two-step exercise. The first thing you'll do is count the number of windows in your house or apartment. Then, partway through your count, I'd like you to say your first name out loud. Got it? Ready? Go.

1. Count the number of windows in your house.
2. While partway through that, say your first name out loud.

What happened to your count when you said your name? It stopped, didn't it? You were able to stop thinking about the windows because you started to think about something else, your name. It wasn't that you just thought about your name, but you said your name out loud. When you speak, your mind stops whatever it is doing and listens. The little engine supplanted self-doubt with positive words. You are able to use words to your advantage as you adopt new attitudes about money.

If you encounter challenges getting one of the new attitudes integrated into your life, then start talking. Take the list of positive thoughts you generated a few minutes ago and say them out loud. If you're at work, maybe take a quick break, go for a walk, and mutter them to yourself under your breath (so no one thinks you're crazy). If you're at home, then stop what you are doing and make yourself say your positive replacement thought out loud.

Understanding the power of the positively spoken word as a way to supplant negative thoughts saved me from surgery after I had my first child. A few hours after my daughter was born, I passed a softball-sized blood clot (sorry if that's too much information), passed out, and then began hemorrhaging. I came to a few minutes later, with the doctor giving me two choices: To rectify the cause of the bleeding, I could go into emergency surgery, which would mean a longer hospital stay and longer postpartum recovery; or she could do a nonsurgical but *extremely* painful procedure.

I opted for the nonsurgical approach. That woman was not kidding when she told me it would be painful. It was excruciating—much worse than childbirth itself. At the first jolt of pain, I wanted to physically resist and push her away from me. I knew I couldn't do that, so I decided to say, "Go, doctor! Go, doctor! You can do it. Go, doctor!" instead.

I knew she was puzzled by my encouraging words while I was in such excruciating pain. After she successfully completed the procedure, I told her, "I used my words to stay focused on the choice I'd made. If I hadn't engaged my mouth, I would have resisted the procedure and then needed surgery."

Positive self-talk is proven to generate positive outcomes. In sports, athletes who use positive self-talk perform better.[1] Positive self-talk has health benefits like a longer life span, greater resistance to the common cold, and decreased chance of death from cardiovascular disease and other medical benefits.[2] It's also the basis for psychological treatment of many conditions, like eating disorders, substance abuse, and chronic back pain.[3] Folks, it works. It works in all these other realms, and it will work for you to develop new attitudes in your finances.

You don't need to wait and react to a negative thought. You can take a proactive approach to this. As awkward as you may feel, say your positive thoughts out loud to yourself a few times each morning. You can orient your thinking to the positive from the start of your day.

Minding Your Attitudes

To a great extent, you are what you think. So if you want to change yourself, you have to change your thoughts. It may feel at times like you have no control over the patterns of your mind, but you do. If you practice talking and thinking in positive ways, little by little you'll notice a difference in the way your mind reacts to the things that happen in your daily life. And before too long, you'll have a brand-new set of attitudes.

8

standing up to pressure

Victorious living does not mean freedom from temptation.

—E. Stanley Jones

*J*ust as Marco and I were about to leave for a Sunday afternoon at a local zoo, I remembered something. "Rats," I said. "We don't have anything to eat." Normally we would grab some concessions as we walked the zoo's grounds, then stop for dinner on the way home. Today, though, we couldn't do that. We made egg salad sandwiches for a picnic lunch, and then headed out to the zoo that afternoon.

Marco and I were in the middle of a thirty-day no-eating-out challenge. We'd forbidden ourselves from spending a dime on any food apart from our regularly scheduled grocery trip. That meant no sit-down restaurants, no fast food, no coffee shops, no lunches out, no snacks from the gas station, no concessions, nothing (except a couple business lunches my sales positions required of me). If we wanted to eat while we were away from home, then we had to pack up the food in advance and bring it with us; we didn't even allow a spur-of-the moment run into the grocery store. The food had to come from inside our house.

It was a grueling challenge for us, but powerfully effective. Over the few months prior to the challenge, we realized that we were spending an insane amount of money eating out. We tried to cut back and curb the habit but failed time and again. Finally we were fed up with our inability to gain mastery in this area and decided to take thirty days off. It was like a detoxification period where we weaned ourselves from a behavior we were not able to control in any other way.

I'm happy to report that we've been able to eat out in moderation ever since we finished the no-eating-out challenge. During the challenge we identified our pressure points and were more clearly able to hear our thoughts about eating out. I realized that I spent most of Thursday and Friday thinking about eating dinner out on Friday night. It wasn't the food that I wanted, but the opportunity to connect with Marco and be around lots of people (I'm a huge extrovert). I learned to redirect my thoughts. We brainstormed alternative solutions, like a barbecue with friends, that met my needs just as well.

On this journey to change your financial life, you will come under pressure. You will desire one thing but feel like something different is the right choice to make. You need to become like a deep-sea creature that has figured out how to withstand the tremendous pressure of the ocean water without collapsing. Let's explore a number of ways that you can do that.

Increase Your Willpower

When I think of willpower, I get the mental image of a tempting desire physically pushing on me, trying to knock me over. Willpower is my fight back against that desire. I resist, pushing and restraining that desire from overcoming me. All the while I am telling myself a thousand no's. I sound like a mom talking to a toddler who is getting into everything. I say "No, don't touch that. No, don't do that. No, don't go there. No, no, no, no!"

Willpower is a very interesting force. It has limitations, but it can be grown and cultivated in our lives. I believe understanding how to develop willpower and knowing what weakens it can help you to stand firmer against temptations.

Think of willpower like a muscle. Through routine exercise you can strengthen your biceps or your heart muscle. Routine displays of willpower will strengthen your willpower muscle. In your physical body you have different muscles that perform distinct functions. Willpower is not like that, with one willpower muscle to help you stop overspending on your kids and another willpower muscle to help you eat more carrots. You've got one "willpower muscle" that influences all the self-control aspects of your life. As you intentionally exert control over your behavior—maybe on something as simple as using your left hand to brush your teeth instead of your right hand—you can strengthen your willpower muscle.[1]

David Blaine, a modern-day Houdini whose stunts involve extreme endurance—like being encased in ice without heavy clothing for nearly three straight days, or spending seven days in a plastic coffin that offered only six inches of excess room[2]—underscores this principle. Blaine attributes his abilities to incredible willpower. In explaining how he's developed such a will, Blaine has said, "Getting your brain wired into little goals, and achieving them, helps you achieve the bigger things you shouldn't be able to do. It's not just practicing the specific thing."[3]

Thankfully, you don't need to hold your breath underwater for over seven minutes like Blaine did.[4] What you need is enough willpower to avoid buying a new large-screen TV after going to a Super Bowl party where you enjoyed your friend's seventy-two-inch screen, or enough to forgo buying things on impulse when you run into the hardware store to pick up a gallon of paint.

Exercising self-control isn't the only thing that is needed to develop willpower. Just like a physical muscle, your willpower muscle needs you to be well rested and well fed. Studies have shown that when people who have slept less than seven hours the night before are required to exercise restraint, they are less able to do so.[5] In a separate study, people who had low glucose levels exhibited less self-control than their counterparts who sipped sugary lemonade.[6] When you find yourself tempted and realize you're hungry, maybe grab a bite to eat, then come back and make your choice.

Beyond physical things, other factors can improve our willpower. Humor and laughter have been found to increase self-control.[7] Similarly, conjuring good memories from times past can improve your mood and your ability to withstand temptation.[8] Like we discussed in the previous chapter, redirecting your thoughts from the immediate situation to a longer-term goal is also an effective strategy.[9]

Willpower's Limitations

Understanding that willpower functions similarly to a physical muscle helps us understand its limitations. Imagine you spent the day working outside at your cabin. You put the dock in the lake. You trimmed trees and hauled wood. You mowed the yard. You weeded the garden. By nightfall you're tired. Your body can only do so much before it runs out of steam. It's the same thing with your willpower muscle. It gets depleted when it is used.[10]

A clear example of this is folks trying to change how they eat. In the morning someone will resist a cinnamon roll for breakfast, then make healthy choices for lunch and an afternoon snack, but by the time the kids are in bed, he's used up all his willpower. The result is a huge bowl of ice cream.

You may find that an occasional giving-in to a temptation you regularly resist could help replenish your willpower. This isn't an excuse for throwing off restraint, but a recognition that always saying no takes effort.

Another potential concern with an ongoing no-no-no thought pattern is the risk that it actually stirs up a desire in you. Like the forbidden fruit in the garden of Eden, the fact that you can't have something can get you started thinking about that thing. Like we discussed in the previous chapter, the more you think about it, the more the desire grows.

Recognize that willpower is a limited resource in your life, and use it wisely. You may not be able to say no to every spending impulse all at once. Doing so will take more willpower than what you've developed. Don't lament that. Instead, prioritize the changes you want to make so that you can focus your willpower on the most important things first. Start with one thing and master that, then move on to the next item on your list.

Avoiding the Temptation

For people trying to quit smoking, the nicotine patch has proven to be a super effective aid. The patch helps eliminate cravings for cigarettes by releasing low levels of nicotine into the wearer's system. These reduced or eliminated cravings have made people who wear the patch twice as likely to quit smoking as those who don't wear one.[11]

In situations where you don't have enough willpower to resist the urge, you are better off eliminating the temptation all together. You may be using up all your willpower on other priorities and don't have enough to successfully change one more behavior. That's when you need to avoid it.

For people who struggle with overspending, I can imagine a set of strategies that includes increasing willpower but also involves avoidance components. You can cancel your credit cards so you are no longer tempted to misuse them. You could switch to a cash-only basis so you don't carry credit or debit cards in your wallet. When your cash runs out, you are done spending. Some years back, a loved one in my life asked me to keep possession of his debit card and checkbook, since he had trouble controlling their use.

Besides eliminating access to easy money, you may want to figure out what triggers your urge or craving. If you find yourself wanting to stop for morning coffee and a bagel every day as you drive past a certain coffee shop, then maybe you need to find a new route to work. Marco and I used to spend Sunday afternoons each spring and fall touring new homes. We weren't in the market to buy, we just enjoyed looking—especially at the multimillion-dollar ones. When we committed to give up I'll-fake-it-'til-I-make-it thinking, our tours of multimillion-dollar homes went with it. The behavior didn't help us and only stirred consumerism desires within us.

As effective as avoidance is, your willpower muscle can atrophy when you don't exercise it. This weakens your ability to make a right choice when the next temptation occurs.

Imagine you did close or cut up all your credit cards. After about a year of successfully changing your financial life, you feel like you've grown to a place where you can handle the cards again. You call to get a replacement for the ones you cut up. A few months after carrying them in your wallet, you notice you've charged more than what you can afford to pay off in a single month. You've started to relapse into your old habit.

Treating avoidance strategies as a short-term solution is the way to address this. Marco and I avoided eating out for thirty days, but we knew we couldn't or wouldn't want to avoid it forever. Our long-term solution had to involve developing the self-control to moderate our behavior. Avoidance was a first step, not a last step, in our process of change.

Tolerate the Stress

I've told you that nicotine patches are effective at helping smokers quit. What if there was something *even more* effective than that? Researchers conducted an experiment where some smokers were given the nicotine patch, while another group of smokers did not get patches, but instead were taught techniques, like deep breathing, to help them tolerate nicotine cravings. The group that learned to tolerate the discomfort of the cravings was twice as likely to quit as those who used patches.[12]

There is something very powerful in what psychologists call *distress tolerance*. At first glance you might think it's synonymous with willpower, but it's not quite. Yes, willpower is required when you withstand any sort of temptation, but distress tolerance isn't your arm-wrestling match with an undesirable urge. It's a counterintuitive approach where you accept and embrace the discomfort.

A classic example is Lamaze classes. Many couples go to some sort of Lamaze or birthing class before having their first child so they know what to expect during labor, and to learn techniques that will make the painful labor contractions tolerable. The woman may learn breathing and mind-focusing techniques. The husband learns to support by introducing other physical stimuli like running ice cubes up and down his wife's arms. These are all distress tolerance techniques that aim at the couple's having a more pleasant labor experience.

I remember hearing the premise for these techniques during the birthing classes I attended. The instructor wanted us to see that labor pains are not a bad thing. Our human nature recoils at the thought of something painful, but in this situation the pain is productive. I was struck with the notion that relaxing and yielding to a contraction can help that contraction be more productive and ultimately reduce the overall duration of your labor.

Distress tolerance is a three-step process:

1. **Acknowledge the discomfort.** You have to acknowledge that discomfort exists. Don't avoid or deny it.
2. **Reframe the discomfort.** To make an uncomfortable thing tolerable, you have to give it some sort of meaning or purpose. Often this involves redirecting your thoughts toward a longer-term goal.
3. **Cope with the discomfort.** Live through the moments of discomfort. You can use a variety of techniques to do this successfully (we'll discuss various techniques in a minute).

When I first heard the phrase *distress tolerance*, I immediately thought of my response to the heat when I lived in the

Peruvian Amazon. The average daily high was 90 degrees, but it felt more like 120 degrees because of the 90 percent humidity level. I'm from Minnesota, where the average high temperature is 55 degrees and the lowest temperature on record is 41 degrees *below zero*.[13] No wonder I found the heat in the Amazon unbearable, especially since I didn't have access to air-conditioning of any sort at any point during the day or night.

During my first few days there, I was bothered by the heat. I was trying to overcome this low-level frustration with a circumstance I couldn't change. My efforts were fruitless. Then it hit me.

The heat was not my problem. The lack of air-conditioning was not my problem. What I hated was feeling sweaty. I was mad because I didn't want to perspire like a lawn sprinkler. Then I went through the three steps to help me tolerate the stress:

1. **I acknowledged that I hated feeling sweaty.** I felt a low-level anger about it that wasn't subsiding but rather growing with each day.
2. **I reframed my discomfort.** I took my focus off the heat and put it on sweatiness. Then I thought about how much I loved the work I was doing and the people whose lives I was influencing. I was willing to put up with sweatiness because I loved everything else so much.
3. **I coped with the discomfort.** I learned to redirect my mind when it would start to focus on the streams of sweat pouring off me. Instead I'd imagine (and sometimes feel it for real) a slight breeze hitting some part of me, and I'd think about the cooling effect being created by the gallons of sweat on my body.

When my mom and other American tourists came to visit me in the Amazon, I helped them tolerate the sweltering heat using these same three steps. It was effective every time.

Coping Techniques

To tolerate discomfort for any amount of time, you need to get yourself to a positive place. A variety of techniques can help you do that. You can pray, use mental imagery, work out, do community service, or a thousand other things. One framework for thinking through the multitude of coping techniques can be thought of using the acronym **ACCEPTS**. Let me explain it with an example.

Imagine you open your mailbox to find one of those letters we hate to get from the bank. The kind that tells you your account is overdrawn. Payday is three days from now, and you aren't sure how you'll get through. Instead of living in a constant state of anxiety for the next three days, use the ACCEPTS techniques to move you to a more positive internal state.[14]

- **Activities.** Spend time over the next few days doing things you really enjoy. If you like to go for walks, then call a friend and schedule a couple. If you enjoy scrapbooking, then pull out your supplies and make a few pages. Not only will the activity keep your mind focused elsewhere, but you can gain a sense of accomplishment or calm when you enjoy your hobbies.

- **Contribute.** Take your eyes off yourself and find a way to give back to someone else. Maybe you have an elderly neighbor who could use a lawn mowing, you can pray for servicemen stationed overseas, or find a local nonprofit that you could help. Giving to others will help you feel better and also distract your mind from ruminating about your problem.

• **Comparisons.** Remember when you were unemployed and went eighteen months without a paycheck? Surely you can get through the next few days. When you were unemployed, you weren't even interested in personal finance, and now you've learned a lot. It's motivating to see how far you've come.

• **Emotions.** Help yourself turn off the anxious and negative emotions by watching a comedy film or playing silly games with your kids.

• **Push away.** You can't shave a minute off the seventy-two hours until payday no matter how much you obsess over your situation. Since you can't change it, there's not much sense in having it consume your time. Find something more urgent to attend to like cooking dinner, cleaning the house, or other simple household tasks.

• **Thoughts.** Identify some replacement thoughts that you can put in your mind each time this bounced check comes to mind. Make positive declarations about yourself and your future out loud.

• **Sensations.** Jerk your mind out of its rut by experiencing a strong physical sensation. Maybe run an ice cube on your arm, or put a rubber band around your wrist and snap it when you sense yourself starting to hyperfocus on the problem. Or maybe you would enjoy a hot shower, a hot cup of tea, or a car ride with the windows down and the sun and wind on your face. Use your physical body to help distract your mind.

Building Your Willpower Muscles

You may think that willpower and pain tolerance are inborn traits that some people have and some people don't. But as we've seen in this chapter, like any other skill set, these abilities can be exercised and enhanced with the right techniques.

Don't be passive, waiting for discomfort and weariness to attack. Prepare yourself ahead of time and then go on the offensive. Fight back!

9

staying in it for the long haul

Pain is temporary. Quitting lasts forever.

—Lance Armstrong

have a purple Weeble on my desk. You know, the plastic children's toy with a weighted round bottom that "wobbles but it won't fall down." I took him out of my daughter's toy box one day when I was on the verge of abandoning my efforts to write this book. It took me seven months to write the first chapter, and then I had six months to write the remaining twelve. I was overwhelmed and afraid.

I was afraid that I couldn't do it. I believed that I was somehow unable to write a book. In hindsight it seems almost silly, because I did do it and it turned out just fine, but I had many anxiety-filled moments during the process.

I think we all have experiences like that at one time or another. We have a responsibility or have made a commitment to something, but it seems beyond reach. We don't know if we are able. We aren't sure if we know the path to take. Worry fills our hearts and minds. At a convenient opportunity, often in sync with a setback of some sort, our motivation is totally lost. We quit.

I have been a lifelong quitter. Somewhere in my childhood I adopted a mind-set that it was better to quit than fail. In situations where I really feared failing, I decided that it was better to not get started at all than fail. In my midtwenties I got fed up with this attitude and my string of undone and unattempted efforts. "The last thing I quit was quitting" became a life slogan for me.

If it weren't for that life slogan and the purple Weeble Wobble as a visual reminder of it, you might not be reading this book right now. As you set out to make changes in your attitudes toward money, it's important that you understand how motivation works, what erodes it, and how to handle setbacks.

Motivation

Motivation is required for you to sustain your effort over the long term. It's especially important when you face some sort of setback or obstacle that works against you. I think of it like a snowplow. In Minnesota, we often get ginormous snowfalls—I remember blizzards where we've gotten twenty inches at a time—and the snowplows push right through the snow to clear the road. The snow may be heavy and wet, but it's no match for the snowplow's strength.

Within us, motivation is a multifaceted force. There are four elements that, when working together properly, help us sustain our effort over time. If you listen to clichés about motivation, you may not get that idea, as they often sound one-dimensional. "Where there's a will, there's a way" or "If you want something badly enough, you'll get it" make it sound like all you need is a desire for the goal and success is inevitable.

If you've ever made a New Year's resolution, then you know it isn't that easy. You really want your life to go in a new direction, but running like a snowplow is hard work. I think that understanding the four factors that most heavily influence motivation will help you stick with your desired financial changes.

The four components are:[1]

- **Commitment.** Commitment is rooted in your sense of purpose. *Why* are you choosing to put effort into making a change to your financial attitudes? Your primary purposes may be process-focused or outcome-focused. You may want to learn to become a better steward of your finances, or you may desire to get out of debt. When you are fueled by a drive to learn or grow via the process, versus aiming for just one concrete goal, you are more able to sustain motivation through tough times.

- **Confidence.** You need to believe you actually can accomplish what you set out to do. When you have previously failed or are doing something you've never done before, then it is more challenging to sustain confidence. Focus on baby steps in the right direction to demonstrate your own ability to yourself. Don't be afraid to look for divine help. I relaxed about my ability to write this book after deciding to trust in a divine ability beyond my own.

- **A sense of Control.** You need to feel like you have the power to bring change. If you think an outside force is keeping your effort from having any impact, it's hard to stay motivated. It's also important to understand how you will get from point A to point B. Seeing a plan or road map can increase your sense of control in the situation.

• **Composure.** You need to operate with a low level of anxiety. Anxiety or worry is nothing more than a nagging, gnawing fear. Over time it will erode your commitment, confidence, and sense of control, leading you to quit. Worry happens in your thoughts and often starts its conversations with the words "what if?" What if you try but fail? What if [insert terrible outcome] happens? It's "what if" after "what if" after "what if." Replace those thoughts with positive ones.

When Setbacks Happen

Now that you understand the dynamics at play when you are highly motivated and on track toward accomplishing your goals, you can better understand what happens when you encounter a setback.

Imagine that you'd been anticipating Christmas this year, setting aside money each month for the gifts you'd be buying. You were eager to have a cash-only holiday and avoid the January doldrums, but as Black Friday approached and you went through the holiday season, you got caught up in the consumerism you'd vowed to avoid. You overspent and blew your budget. It's too late to return anything to the store, as gifts are opened and kids are excited about their new toys. How does a mistake like this impact your motivation?

• **Commitment.** You'd wanted to have so much debt paid off before the New Year, but that won't happen. Since you won't reach that goal, you wonder why you should keep trying.

- **Confidence.** You were just starting to feel like you were getting ahead financially, but now you wonder if you can trust yourself with money. You aren't sure if you'll ever get your finances straightened out.

- **A sense of Control.** You did fine until you went shopping with your mom and sisters. Although they didn't do anything overt, it's like their presence created a peer pressure for you to buy more. You can't escape family. How will you live a disciplined life if you have to interact with them all the time?

- **Composure.** Where is the money going to come from for your January credit card bill? You hadn't planned on those expenses, and now you've got to siphon money from somewhere else.

Maybe you didn't blow your budget, but got laid off or had an emergency that was bigger than your small but growing emergency fund. Think through your self-talk in these four areas with whatever challenge you face to get a pulse on your motivation.

You can see how a slip-up, mistake, intentional sabotage, or other undesirable event can momentarily shake your motivation. That's normal. Just don't let it entice you into throwing in the towel.

Resilience

Resilience is what it takes to keep going even when you've encountered an obstacle. Commonly we say it's an ability to bounce back. But not like a rubber band that stretches and then returns to its original shape. We're more like clay whose shape or form gets molded when we encounter pressure.

Resilience almost always involves adaptation. In that way, I think of it more like one of those super-resistant strains of bacteria I hear about on the news. The bacteria has been over-exposed to antibiotics and adapted as a result. The bacteria has become so strong through its adaptation that doctors fear we may not have a medicine powerful enough to stop it.

This adaptation happens in a process over time through repeated exposure to obstacles (antibiotics). Our own resilience happens in a process and isn't an inherited trait like blue eyes or curly hair, according to Rick Newman, author of the book *Rebounders: How Winners Pivot from Setback to Success.* Newman says that resilience, above intelligence, sets the world's most successful people apart from others mainly because individuals can increase their resilience, whereas intelligence largely can't be changed.[2]

Reframing

Like a kaleidoscope, *reframing* is turning your view of the perceived setback just slightly to get an entirely different picture. As Michael Jordan, the basketball legend, said in a Nike commercial, "I've missed more than nine thousand shots in my career. I've lost almost three hundred games. Twenty-six times, I've been trusted to take the game-winning shot and missed. I've failed over and over and over again in my life. And that is why I succeed." He has taken what others may call "failures" and adopted a perspective where those things are instruments of success. He understands the power of reframing setbacks.

Start with your purpose

Your starting point in the reframing process needs to be your commitment. But be aware that a single mistake or setback can seem fatal if you are bore-sighted on one particular outcome. It's better to have your motivational purpose be process-oriented. If you're committed to development, to learning, or to growing, there is room for missteps and "Whoops! I wish I hadn't done that" decisions.

Continuing with our Christmas gifts example, maybe your primary purpose for changing your financial attitudes could be a commitment to model good stewardship to your children. Certainly paying off a certain amount of debt is a fine secondary goal. I'm cautioning you from making an outcome-focused result your primary driving force.

Reframe for each component of motivation

You've started with your commitment, but it's important to carry the reframing through to the other components of motivation. Look at the list below to see how you can reframe the overspending on gifts.

- **Commitment.** I want to teach my kids good stewardship, but I just indulged them and overspent to do it. I think they're old enough for me to explain indulgence to them, then help them find some old toys they can give away to charity.
- **Confidence.** I did overspend, but I have less debt this Christmas than in recent memory. I did an excellent job setting aside a little bit each month to have for the holidays.

- **A sense of Control.** I need to do a better job setting my own personal spending limits in advance. Maybe next year I can get a prepaid debit card loaded with the money I have to spend, then when it is gone, it's gone.
- **Composure.** I wish I'd be able to pay off the bill in January, but I'm not going to be able to. I'll have to incur some interest on it. It's not my ideal, but it isn't the end of the world. Next year I'll do even better.

You can see why resilient people are able to keep moving, even after they've stumbled. Their self-talk is more positive and supportive of their desire to make change. Overly critical self-talk drains your energy.

Learn from your mistake

Setbacks and apparent failures can be instructive learning opportunities when you see them as an inoculation that will ultimately make you stronger. Thomas Edison is one of the most prolific inventors of the modern age. He holds more than a thousand patents, which ranks him among the top patent holders in human history. His inventions didn't happen without a series of failed attempts. Edison is credited as saying, "I've not failed. I've just found ten thousand ways that won't work."[3]

Not only did Edison reframe his setbacks, but he learned from them and went on to develop things like the phonograph, the first commercially reproducible incandescent light bulb, the carbon microphone used in all telephones along with the Bell receiver until the 1980s, and the system for the generation and distribution of electricity.[4] Likewise, we need to stop at each setback, take an objective look at what went well and what went wrong, then learn from those lessons.

Recognize that "You've already paid the tuition so why not get the learning," as Paul Schoemaker, author of *Brilliant Mistakes* (Wharton, 2011), has said.[5]

As you reflect on your setback, try to learn more than what the mistake cost you. That will make it an asset and not a liability.[6] Be objective versus emotional and think through questions like these (you can add your own questions; this is just a starting list):

- What went well?
- What didn't work so well?
- What was frustrating about the situation? What changes can I make to avoid that frustration in the future?
- Based on how things went, what should I start doing from now on? Or what should I do more of?
- What should I stop doing or do less of?
- What lessons did I learn through this event?

Your answers to those questions will only be instructive and useful if you are willing to accept an appropriate level of personal responsibility. Blame is a very real temptation. When I'm tempted to say that someone or something else is my problem, I think of Jim Collins' explanation of the window and the mirror in his book *Good to Great*.[7] Collins says that corporate leaders who turned good companies into great companies looked in the mirror to accept responsibility for bumps in the road. They looked out the window to generously distribute credit when success happened. Interestingly, leaders in other good companies that stagnated at good or even fizzled out did just the opposite. They looked out the window to assign blame when setbacks occurred, but quickly looked in the mirror to take credit for any success.

Be good to yourself

Looking at mistakes in a positive light can be difficult. I encourage you throughout the process of reframing and learning from what's happened to treat yourself well. Extend to yourself the same compassion you'd extend to someone else.[8]

1. **Notice your own hurt.** It's okay to acknowledge your feelings about a setback. You don't have to pretend.
2. **Be kind to yourself.** Encourage yourself the same way you'd encourage a friend who told you about a mistake she made at work. You'd help her regain footing, not beat her up. Do the same for yourself.
3. **Recognize that missteps make you human.** Making a poor choice or experiencing a tragic event are common human experiences. You aren't alone. If you were talking with a struggling friend, you might remind him of a time you struggled so he wouldn't feel isolated and alone.

Keep Moving

The old adage "Put one foot in front of the other" rings true when it comes to resilience. Rick Newman, author of *Rebounders: How Winners Pivot from Setback to Success* (Ballantine, 2012), says that all rebounders are resilient; they may have experienced a struggle of some sort, but they kept moving.[9] You need to keep moving too.

After experiencing a setback, find an opportunity for success. Then take it. Seeing yourself do something positive will boost your confidence, revitalize your commitment, give you a sense of control, and help squelch fear. It breathes new life into your motivation.

Choosing to swing the bat again is especially difficult for people who struggle with perfectionist tendencies. I can fall that way and understand how a combination of excessively high standards and overly critical self-talk can impede me from acting. I've learned, though, that pushing through and doing something—anything positive—helps.

Imagine how each of these well-known people felt when they heard crushing words about their talent.

- Oprah Winfrey was fired from a reporter's position at Baltimore's WJZ-TV. The producer said she was "unfit for television."[10]
- After one performance at the Grand Ole Opry, the concert hall's manager told Elvis Presley that he was better off returning to his old career of truck driving.[11]
- Walt Disney was fired by a newspaper editor because "he lacked imagination and had no good ideas."[12]
- Feedback after Fred Astaire's first test included, "Can't act. Slightly bald. Also dances."[13]
- After auditioning for a contract with Decca Records, the Beatles were told they "have no future in show business" and "guitar groups are on the way out."[14]

I'd be stung to hear such critical words, and I am sure they were too. But these people didn't let those stinging words be the last ones. They took another step, then another, and another, and came back stronger than ever.

now that you're ready, some simple budgeting advice

*T*he main focus of this book has been on changing your attitudes toward money—not on teaching you how to build a budget. To some extent, this is the book you should read *before* you get into the nitty-gritty of financial planning.

That being said, it is helpful to know what kind of plan is right for you and, once you choose one, how to use it most effectively. The next few chapters give some general advice. We'll cover how to think about your spending plan (which is a phrase I like to use instead of *budget*—I'll explain in the next chapter). Chapter 11 is dedicated to the how-to's of paying off debt. In chapter 12 we talk about how to hold yourself accountable. And in the final chapter, I'll share some helpful money-saving tips from my own research and experience.

Laid on top of a solid set of attitudes, these practical things will make a tremendous impact on your financial life.

10

creating a spending plan

If you've ever tried to lose weight, then the word *diet* likely makes you cringe. A diet represents everything you can't eat. In much the same way, I don't like the word *budget*. A budget represents everything I can't do. It tells me everything I can't spend money on. It constrains me from having fun on a Friday night because "Oh yeah, I'm on a budget now. I can't afford to go out to eat or to a movie anymore." No wonder I'd never kept a budget, although I'd made many of them over the years. Instead, I prefer a *spending plan*.

A spending plan, on paper anyway, might look an awful lot like a budget. It's a layout of how much you make and how you intend to spend the money you have. But it's different from a budget. A spending plan is permission-centered, not constraint-centered. You create a spending plan because you want to, well, plan to spend. It allows you to decide your spending priorities before you have an emotional buzz seeing a large balance in your checking account on payday. It's not about what you cannot do, but a reflection of what you can and will do with every penny of your money. As you make planful choice after planful choice, you'll see your money accomplish far more than you dreamed possible.

Types of Expenses

To create your spending plan, you need to understand the three types of expenses that occur in life. Every good and service in your life falls into one of three categories:

- **Predictable monthly expenses.** These are the needs we talked about in chapter 4, "It Won't Happen to Me." I'd also encourage you to allocate money toward "treats" so they become predictable monthly expenses.
- **Predictable non-routine expenses.** These are the goals we talked about in chapter 4.
- **Unpredictable expenses.** These are things you have no way to plan for—bona fide emergencies—but need to set money aside for anyway.

We need to understand these different types of expenses and take an honest look at how much each costs so we can plan for them.

Type #1: Predictable Monthly Expenses

Your predictable monthly expenses are the easiest to understand. These expenses are important to your daily survival, as they cover many basic needs like food, shelter, and transportation. These expenses are probably not hindering your financial progress. You likely judge whether something is affordable by looking at it in the light of your current load of monthly bills. These expenses stare you in the face every single month.

Even within this category of routine pay-them-each-month expenses, there are two types. The first are those whose payment remains constant each month, like your mortgage or your cell phone bill. We'll call these **fixed monthly expenses**, since the payment is, like the name implies, fixed. Fixed monthly expenses are like a fastball down the middle. You know they are coming. They hit you right where you expect them every time.

Other monthly expenses have payment amounts that vary month-to-month. We'll call these **variable monthly expenses**. These are more like curveballs. You see them coming, but they sometimes take an unexpected turn and catch you off guard. Things like utility bills, groceries, gasoline, and eating out fall into this category.

Type #2: Predictable Non-Routine Expenses

Non-routine, predictable expenses are the classic budget busters we talked about in chapter 4. They are the expenses we work hard at pretending aren't going to cost us money—from new brakes to new eyeglasses to a new winter coat, and summer vacations to holiday entertaining to three baby showers over the span of six weeks.

I've included a list of all sorts of things that would qualify as predictable non-routine expenses. My list is not all-inclusive; no list really can be because our non-routine expenses are as varied as our personalities, hobbies, interests, and family structures. Use my list as a starting point to jog your thinking, but then look at the list of goals you made in chapter 4 and reflect back over the past year to everything you spent money on. Look ahead too, to the next month, three months, and even twelve to eighteen months, and imagine everything you and your family will want or need in that time frame. All those things taken together—looking forward and backward—are your predictable non-routine expenses.

Potential Non-Routine Expenses

- Clothing
- Car maintenance
- Car repairs
- Dental expenses
- Gifts
- Haircuts, color, and other salon services
- Hosting parties and events
- House repairs and home improvement projects
- House maintenance
- Jewelry and accessories
- Family outings, date nights, recreation
- Insurance for car and home
- Kids' activities like swimming lessons, baseball, and dance lessons
- Lawn care and maintenance
- Medical expenses
- Newspaper and magazine subscriptions
- Office supplies like copy paper and toner
- Orthodontist expenses
- Shoes
- Sports equipment and gym memberships
- Supplies for hobbies
- Travel
- Vacations
- Water bill

Type #3: Unpredictable Expenses

I told you about Marco's dad passing away unexpectedly on Christmas morning 2006 and Marco's $2,000 plane ticket home to Rio de Janeiro. That was a bona fide emergency. There is no reasonable way we could have foreseen that trip and planned our finances to specifically accommodate it. Unexpected expenses are wild pitches that make you holler "Heads up!" and take cover to avoid being hit by a ball coming out of nowhere.

A Starting-Point Snapshot

Now it's time for you to get to work. No, I don't want you to create a balanced budget. That's not your goal right now. The first thing you need to do is figure out how much your current lifestyle costs. You need to come completely clean with yourself, and your spouse, about what you have been spending your money on and how much of it you have been spending. With such easy access to credit and debt, you may have lost sight of how much you are truly spending compared with how much you earn.

If you purpose to create a balanced budget at this point, then you'll skew all your expenses down just to make the numbers work. You want to believe that you are living within your means. We all do. But you may not be. You have to understand the magnitude of change that is being required of you, or else you'll underestimate the effort needed for success. An honest, albeit shocking and even scary starting-point snapshot is a step in the right direction.

Something shocking happened to Marco and me when we took a snapshot of our lifestyle in June 2006. Our fully loaded, included-every-predictable-non-routine-expense-we-spent-money-on expense level was nearly $2,000 more per month than our income. That was a brutal slap in the face. After paying our bills each pay period, we seemed to have more than enough. There was almost always some money left over. Yet the black-and-white numbers of our starting-point snapshot told a different story. I looked at that little bit as extra, when in reality it was lack.

Marco and I considered ourselves responsible, non-extravagant folks, yet we lacked the money to cover all our predictable non-routine expenses. We were living thousands of dollars per month beyond our means. We hit our monthly bills out of the park and didn't ever miss paying those; it was everything else in life that was beyond what we could afford. Marco and I had appointed me as captain of our financial ship, and our ship was sinking. The worst part was I didn't even realize it. Sobering.

A From-Scratch Spending Plan

After doing a starting-point snapshot, Marco and I knew that our lifestyle was out of whack with our income—to the tune of a few thousand dollars each month. It was time for us to make a spending plan, and associated savings plans, that we could live with on a day-to-day basis and that would protect us from future debt.

The process we went through was like cleaning the closet in a child's bedroom. You know the process—you pull everything out, make a huge mess, then look at each item and only put the most important things back inside. When you choose to put things back inside the closet, you only do so if you have a place for the item. That was us with our finances.

We started with a clean slate and called no expense sacred. Everything, and I mean e-v-e-r-y-t-h-i-n-g, was negotiable. In times past, our primary financial priority was to meet our monthly obligations. Our new priority was to save for bona fide emergencies.

An Emergency Fund

Financial planners everywhere agree on the need for families to have cash on hand that would cover three to six months' worth of expenses should tragedy strike. The concept of setting aside money for emergencies wasn't new, but our commitment to actually do it was. We agreed to start saving 10 percent of our income toward the goal of having $12,000 on hand to use in a legitimate emergency.

We started saving in June 2006, so when the dreaded phone call came on Christmas morning that my father-in-law had died, we did not have to worry about how we'd pay for the trip. Marco flew home to Brazil and took unpaid time off of work, but we didn't miss a financial beat because we had money in our emergency fund to cover those expenses.

The trick to actually saving 10 percent of our income was to outsmart our two sabotaging tendencies—spending the money before we could get it into savings, and moving the money right back out of savings for non-emergency purposes.

Here's how we did it:

1. We opened up a new bank account at an online bank

Online banks don't have brick-and-mortar branches. You link your online bank account to your primary account so that deposits and withdrawals are made by transferring funds between them. (ING Direct is the online bank we use, but there are others as well.)

165

2. We scheduled an autotransfer of 10 percent of our income to happen every payday

We knew that if we had a bill worth 10 percent of our income, we'd find a way to pay it. We treated our savings the same way by scheduling the withdrawal to happen routinely and automatically. That made us account for it and kept us from spending the money before it could be saved.

3. We limited our ability to withdraw funds

With most online banks, you have a couple ways you can get money out of your account. You can get a debit-type card or old-fashioned checks, or you can transfer funds into the linked bank account from another bank. We know our tendency to take money back out of savings, so we have never had a debit card or checkbook for our emergency fund account.

When we need money out of it, we have to schedule the transfer online. It doesn't just happen instantaneously; it takes at least three business days for the transfer to occur, which is much better than the immediate transfer that happens when your savings and checking are at the same bank. Since we can't get the money for at least three days, we can't use our emergency fund to cover pseudo-emergencies caused by poor cash-flow planning. It's for *real* life-and-death-type emergencies, not bounced checks. Our savings is just to save.

Monthly Predictable Expenses

After our emergency fund, our next set of financial priorities was our monthly predictable expenses. You can reference our spending plan template at PocketYourDollars.com/Spending -Plan to see what we included as predictable monthly expenses, but it is all your standard stuff—mortgage, debt payments, utilities, gasoline, etc. (more on debt payments in the next chapter). Our family is deeply committed to charitable giving, so we included our charitable giving as a monthly expense. The entire time we were getting out of debt, we gave away over 10 percent of our gross income. We simply adjusted our expenses elsewhere to accommodate it.

Predictable Non-Routine Expenses

Our third priority in our spending plan were the predictable non-routine expenses. I don't put them in third place because they are less important than the others; they're not. I don't put them in third place because they aren't needed; they are. These are the group of expenses that are most flexible, which is why we addressed them last.

We knew we needed to set aside money every month for all the non-routine things that come up in life, but we had a lot of discretion over the amount we set aside. Remember, we had to shave $2,000 per month off our expenses—or we had to increase our income via a second job, which neither of us wanted to do—in order to make our spending plan work.

This time, with this plan, we didn't just give lip service to the numbers we put down. We committed ourselves to put forth whatever amount of effort was needed to actually live out the numbers we agreed upon. The first couple rounds of expense cutting weren't too hard. All the obvious you-don't-fit-in-our-financial-plan-anymore expenses came off—cable, magazine subscriptions, highlights for my hair, trips to most anywhere, new throw pillows, and other nonessential items.

Then we got to the place where we knew it would hurt. In order to prioritize our emergency fund savings and our

167

monthly expenses, we had to figure out how to live our life on significantly less money. Throughout the conversations Marco and I had, I often heard the voice of a former co-worker in my mind. She and her husband had both been laid off in the economic downturn that started in the year 2000. When my company hired her, she was amazed that her family had made it through. They had not lost their home, but they had used up most of their savings just trying to make ends meet. Poignantly, she commented that she never knew she could live without paper towels until it was required of her.

I'd think of her and her dishrags that replaced paper towels. When she and her husband were forced to reduce expenses to a bare minimum, they did it. If she could do it, then Marco and I could do it too.

We talked through our plans, wants, and needs for the months ahead and laid out numbers that would move us toward that future without requiring us to go into debt. But like anything, a plan is useless if you don't walk it out. Again, we needed to find a way to actually save the money that we'd dedicated in our spending plan for non-routine expenses.

We followed a similar three-step process like we'd done for our emergency fund.

1. We opened up a new bank account at a different bank

I would have been fooling myself to think that I could build a nest egg of any sort in a savings account attached to my checking account. I'd tried it dozens of times and failed every single one. I could not trust myself; therefore, I needed to create some distance between me and my money. We opened a new checking account in a different bank than the institution where we had our primary checking account. Yes, this is our third bank account, but this is not an everyday account; this new account's sole purpose is to pay for our non-routine expenses.

2. We scheduled an autotransfer of the lump-sum total of our non-routine expenses once per month

To force ourselves to set aside money for our non-routine expenses, we had to automate the process. We completed the paperwork to establish an ACH transfer (like a direct deposit) from our primary checking account into our secondary checking account once per month. The deposit was a lump-sum total of what we figured out were our non-routine expenses.

We treated this monthly payment like a bill. It could not be stopped or reversed on impulse, the way online transfers can be stopped with the push of a button. The only way to end the ACH transfer was for us to complete another form at a branch of the primary bank a few days before the transfer would happen.

Although we made a lump-sum monthly deposit into this account, we didn't think of it as one large slush fund. The deposit had money earmarked for various categories. We kept an Excel worksheet updated with deposits and withdrawals by category. That meant we could have money in the overall checking account but not have any earmarked for new clothes. Our choices then were to go without new clothes that month, find a legal way to get free clothes, or borrow money from another account with a repayment plan.

3. We made it somewhat painful to get the money out

When we talked about saving money for these non-routine expenses, both Marco and I could foresee a problem. We could imagine ourselves justifying the things we wanted and reaching for these funds to cover our impulses and whims. We needed to protect ourselves against our own impulsivity.

As a result, we chose a small credit union with a limited number of branches, a limited number of ATM machines, and limited hours. Our plan for this savings account for non-routine expenses was to decide in advance what we might need, figure out how much it would cost, and physically go to the bank to get the money for it. We skipped getting debit cards but did allow ourselves old-fashioned ATM cards, since the branch had such limited hours.

Results

Six years ago we started managing our money to account for the full range of expenses in life. The day we started this we were deeply in debt. But day after day, month after month, our savings balances grew and our debt load decreased.

No rich uncle has died and no bags of money have fallen from heaven over the years. Yet since we started living by a spending plan and an associated savings plan, we've done all these things in six years without having borrowed a dime:

- Sent Marco to Brazil when his dad died
- Bought a three-year-old Toyota Sienna minivan
- Paid for Marco's graduate school program
- Put a brand-new furnace in our house
- Spent an overnight in the hospital with our eighteen-month-old daughter
- Sent our six-week-old daughter to the hospital via ambulance
- Had three dental crowns

- Bought all new appliances for our kitchen (twice)
- Paid $3,000 for an unexpected lawyer's bill
- Put new tires on our car
- Replaced the carpet in our home
- Wrote a check at closing for $24,000 to sell our townhouse without a short sale

Before you dismiss this list as impossible for you because you think we must have some sky-high income, let me correct you. We don't. We have accomplished all these things without debt because we have planned and saved for them in advance.

No Yo-Yo Budgeting

I began this chapter by comparing a budget to a diet. If we look more closely at that comparison, we can see even more ways in which these things are similar. Just like when you're choosing an eating and exercise plan, you want to choose a spending plan that you'll stick with over time rather than one you'll try for a few weeks and then give up on. You want one that is flexible enough to work around numerous changes in circumstances. And you want one, first and foremost, that works.

Diets with long-term results, such as Weight Watchers, focus more on what you *can* eat than on what you *can't*. It's not a matter of figuring out what you won't be allowed to have anymore in your life. It's a matter of making the very most of what you *do* have.

11

paying off debt

Imagine that you set a goal to get out of debt. You are full of energy to pay it all off. Your plan: Put every extra penny beyond your basic needs toward debt. Your reasoning: It'll be paid off in no time. You set out on this quest to eliminate credit card debt, car loans, and student loans.

You make an absolutely bare-bones budget. After all, you figure that if you can live on very little for the next few years, then you'll have more each month to put toward repaying debt obligations. You even sell a few things on eBay and put that money directly toward your debt.

Things go along fine for a few months, until you run over a nail and pop a tire. The tire shop recommends you replace all four tires, but at a minimum you have to replace two of them. Uh-oh. Your bare-bones budget was steeped in it-won't-happen-to-me thinking and didn't allow for you to save any money for this sort of thing. Frustrated, you charge the tires.

Adding that few hundred dollars to your supposed-to-be-diminishing debt load is deflating. For months you had been scrimping by so that you could get out of debt quickly, but you fell right back into it. Now you're faced with some additional temptations. Like an alcoholic who falls off the wagon, you think it might be time to splurge on some treats, since you certainly deserve them after having been so tight with money lately.

Over the course of a few weeks, you've re-racked up all the debt you've worked hard to eliminate over the previous few months. You lost all your momentum to get out of debt. This sad downward spiral started with just one setback that you could have avoided.

Financial Priorities

It's dangerous ground to set "I want to get out of debt" as an exclusive, overarching financial goal. The danger is that you'll likely overemphasize paying off your current debts at the exclusion of saving money to avoid incurring new debt.

That's why, when Marco suggested we get out of debt in June 2006, I said I'd agree, but only on one condition. I'd agree to get out of debt if he would agree that we would stay out of debt for the rest of our lives. This goal requires proper financial priorities. The first goal is to create a buffer between you and the need for future debt. Second, you'll pay back the money you owe as quickly as possible.

If you are on a sinking boat, you first plug the leak, then bail the water. Living by a well-thought-out spending plan is your first line of defense in avoiding future debt. Your spending plan calls on you to save a portion of your money for bona fide emergencies and non-predictable expenses. You have to

174

be serious about saving money for future expenses before you get serious about paying back what you've already borrowed.

It's Time to Pay Off Debt

Once Marco and I set our eyes to pay back all the money we'd borrowed to date, it didn't take nearly as long as I'd expected. We used an approach commonly called the debt snowball, or rollover method, as our debt repayment plan. Using the debt snowball plan, you will pay off your lowest balance loans first without regard to interest rate. This approach allows you to get some quick wins and reduce the overall number of outstanding loans you have. It's all about motivation. See, we're not machines; we're human beings. You turn on a machine with the flip of a switch. With us, yeah, we don't have a switch that makes us go. Motivation is our fuel to accomplishing goals. We work when we are motivated to work.

I hear you that mathematically you could pay less overall interest if you organized your debts by interest rates, from high to low. However, that mathematical calculation assumes you won't quit along the way because you run out of steam paying off a $17,000 credit card balance first. We all know that goals are supposed to be measurable and achievable. If your debt is large, like ours was, then it doesn't really feel achievable when you start. It didn't to me, anyway.

We started living by a spending plan and started a debt snowball process, but I never *really* thought we'd be out of debt. It didn't seem plausible that I could be one of those debt-free people. But as we started to pay off a few small debts—five hundred dollars to a family member and a small balance on a store-issued credit card—my confidence grew.

175

"Maybe, just maybe," I thought, "we can pay all these loans off." Then, when we avoided debt during our next bona fide emergency, my confidence soared. Small win after small win after small win.

Psychologists have proven the effectiveness of this debt snowball plan. Researchers set out to understand why people would pay off loans with the smallest balance first, regardless of what the interest rates are. They discovered that consumers have "debt account aversion." That's a fancy name for the sense of being overwhelmed with lots of loans from many different lenders.[1] We feel better when we have fewer outstanding balances. That positive energy fuels our momentum to pay off the next debt and the one after that.

With the debt snowball, you pay the minimum amount on every debt you have. Yes, that means if you have been making something more than the minimum payment, you can stop doing that for now. Then, when you get a little extra money from somewhere—whether you sell some things on craigslist, work overtime, or do odd jobs for someone—you apply that money to the one debt that is at the top of your list. You put every extra cent toward paying off that debt.

Eventually you will pay off that first debt. When you do pay it off, resist telling yourself, "Ahhh, now we don't have to make that debt payment anymore, so we have a little more breathing room in our budget." Instead, apply the minimum payment that you were making for that debt to your next debt. Get it? "Snowball" the minimum payments into one another.

Now you are making more than the minimum payment on your second debt. When that's paid off, then you snowball the entire monthly amount you were paying there into your next debt. You continue on down the line until every penny you've borrowed is paid back.

Your Debt Pay-Off Plan

To get started with your own debt snowball:

1. Make a list of every debt you have

Include the name of the creditor, the outstanding balance on the account, and the minimum monthly payment. Be sure to include debts to family and friends as well as credit cards, student loans, car loans, lines of credit, and every other outstanding loan you have. Whether you include your mortgage debt is up to you. I'll discuss more about this at the end of the chapter.

2. Order your debts by balance

Like we discussed, prioritize your debts with the lowest-balance items at the top of the list. Remember, the reason isn't mathematical but emotional. You'll make more overall progress more quickly than if you ordered debts by interest rate.

3. Make minimum payments on every debt

You may have been trying to accelerate the payoff of some debts by paying more than the minimum payment required. Right now focus on paying the minimum monthly amount due to every single creditor.

4. Get laser-focused on the lowest-balanced debt

Now you can start putting every extra penny toward debt. This isn't the same as the example from earlier, when you put everything toward debt but then had to charge new car tires. Now you have a spending plan in place that has you saving for the future and saving for emergencies, and you are making minimum payments on every debt. Any additional money that comes in—whether a pay increase, a gift, or freed-up cash because you paid off a debt—becomes additional money on your quest to get out of debt.

What's the Snowball?

It's this laser focus, especially with the freed-up cash you get every time you pay off a debt, that gives this approach its name. Let's talk through an example I've laid out in the chart below.

Debt	Balance	Interest Rate	Minimum Payment	Snowball Payment
1. Credit card #1	$750	12%	$19	
2. Credit card #2	$1,500	15%	$42	$61 ($19 + $42)
3. Car loan	$6,000	1%	$350	$411 ($61 + $350)
4. Credit card #3	$17,200	17%	$67	$478 ($411 + $67)
5. Student loan	$22,000	5%	$280	$758 ($478 + $280)

Your first debt is credit card #1 with a balance of $750, and a minimum monthly payment of $19. You pick up some overtime at work, put the $50 your dad gave you for Christmas and the proceeds from a garage sale toward that debt and pay it off in record time—just a few months after you start on this journey.

Now, instead of absorbing that $19 back into your monthly cash flow and spending it on who knows what or saving it in your emergency fund, you keep it dedicated toward debt. You add the $19 minimum payment from credit card #1 to the $42 per month minimum payment you are making on credit card #2. Added together, that's $61 per month—the new minimum payment on your second debt.

Again, you keep up those $61-per-month payments and direct any truly extra money toward that second credit card. In time, you'll get it paid off as well. Again, you avoid absorbing that $61 into your monthly cash flow and snowball it into the minimum payment on your next debt.

You can see in the chart above that by the time you are focused on paying off your $22,000 in student loans, your snowballed minimum payment will be $758 every single month. That's over three times the required minimum payment. That kind of focused effort causes your debt to melt away.

Dedicated Stream of Income

While we were getting out of debt, Marco worked as an international sales rep for a local sign company. Like most salesmen, he made a modest base salary but earned a significant amount in commissions on top of that. When we were first married, we treated that commission check as part of our regular monthly income. Then, a few years later, when we made a significant commitment to our church's stewardship campaign, we decided to dedicate 100 percent of Marco's commission toward fulfilling that obligation.

In June 2006, when we decided to get out of debt and stay out of debt forever, we went back to living on the income from those commission checks again. But we decided to do something radical. We agreed to live on my income and Marco's base salary alone—including funding our emergency fund and saving for all of our financial goals—and dedicate his commission to debt repayment.

Let me be clear that it seemed impossible at the start. I mean, simply meeting our needs seemed to require the commission checks, and even then we found ourselves sometimes relying on credit. How would we live life, build an emergency fund, and save money for our future goals without using that commission check? In a million creative ways we reduced our expenses—and I mean r-a-d-i-c-a-l-l-y reduced our expenses—to make it happen.

You may not have a monthly commission check, but you likely have some other income stream that you can devote to debt repayment. You may already have a job, even a part-time or intermittent job, that you could devote to this purpose. If not, it may be a good time to think about how you can make a few extra dollars and put 100 percent of that money toward the debt you are currently focused on. If nothing else, set aside your "found money" for that purpose. "Found money" comes from refunds, rebate checks, gifts, and other totally unexpected, unplanned places.

Limiting Access to Credit Cards

Now that you've committed to a lifestyle free from debt, you don't need a wallet full of credit cards. I'm not opposed to carrying one free, no-annual-fee major credit card to use for online purchases and things like car rentals. But apart from that one card, work to close every other account (see word of caution below). Decide now that you won't open any new ones. Sure, you'll be tempted when the cashier offers you a 10 percent savings when you open a store charge card, but resist. Not only do you spend more when you pay via credit card,[2] you don't need "members only" coupons and additional advertising in your mailbox.

If you are going to live a life without debt, then you don't need ready access to all that debt. One card will get you through.

You may find it tempting to pull out the card when you know that cash is tight in your checking account. If it's a mental struggle for you, then leave the card at home. If even that isn't enough, I'd encourage you to put your credit card in a one-gallon zip-top bag filled with water. Then put the whole thing into your freezer and let it sit. You can access the card in a bona fide emergency, but it'll take so long to get out of that ice block that you can't use it on impulse.

Word of caution about closing accounts: You need to know that closing a number of your credit cards while still carrying a balance on them can negatively impact your credit score. Similarly, opening up a store charge card, paying it off, and closing it right away can hurt your credit score.[3]

Credit bureaus also look at something called *utilization,* which considers how much debt you have compared to the sum total of credit lines available to you. For instance, if you have two credit cards each with a $5,000 credit limit, then you have a total credit line of $10,000. If you carry a $4,000 balance between them, then you have a 40 percent utilization rate. If you close one of those credit cards, then your available credit line decreases to $5,000, but your balance remains at $4,000, which is an 80 percent utilization rate. That higher utilization rate receives a lower credit score.[4] As you pay down your debt, then your utilization rate decreases and your credit score improves again. You'll need to decide when it makes sense for you to close all but one of your major credit card accounts.

Lower Your Interest Rates

As you set out to pay off debt, do yourself this favor: Attempt to lower your interest rates. Although your debts aren't prioritized by interest rate, that doesn't mean you're oblivious to the fact that the more interest you pay, the longer it will take to repay your loan.

Credit cards—whose interest rates are typically astronomical—are a great place to try to get lower rates. If you've been a long-term customer and have a solid repayment history, then you may be able to negotiate a lower rate.

A Word About Mortgages

There are two ways to look at your debt when creating your debt snowball plan. You can include your mortgage as a debt, because it is one, and use the debt snowball until you've paid it off. Or you can do as Marco and I did and take a break from your debt snowball when you've repaid everything except your mortgage.

It's your choice about how you want to position your mortgage, but I want to explain the reason Marco and I excluded it from our debt snowball. During the time we focused on paying down debt, we stopped contributing to our retirement accounts (which were very meager anyway), but we were not getting any younger. After paying off all our non-mortgage debt, we had two financial goals: (1) we needed to save for a new vehicle, which was not cheap; and (2) we had to prioritize long-term savings for our children's educations and our own retirement.

It was at that point when we first met with a financial planner and started to map our financial future. We discussed the kinds of investments we want; the risk we can tolerate; and our long, long-range life goals and plans. Then we figured out how much money we needed to set aside toward that each month.

It's as if we added "retirement" and "helping our children through college" to our list of goals at that point. We started to actively save toward those goals. Our focus was that every penny that came in above and beyond what we set as a savings goal for those long-range items would be used to pay off our mortgage. Our goal is to pay off our mortgage by the time Marco is sixty, which is October 2025.

12

holding yourself accountable

*I*magine that you are on the board of directors for a large corporation. You fly into town for a quarterly board meeting. The company's CEO opens the meeting with a PowerPoint presentation. He reminds the board of the organization's strategy and vision for the future, then gets specific about the quarterly goals—many of them financial in nature—that the company has worked toward.

He wraps up his presentation, but he left something out or you missed it. He didn't talk about how the company performed financially and whether they met the goals. You speak up about it. "Thanks for the presentation. One thing I'm still curious about is how the company actually performed. Can you share some financial figures that help us see our profitability over the last quarter?"

The CEO responds, "I keep track of the organization's budget and spending in my head. I can certainly jot down my sense of where things are, but I don't have anything to print off and show you that firmly describes how we've been doing financially."

If a CEO did this in real life, he'd be fired immediately. The stock market requires earnings or profit reports four times each year from publicly traded companies. We expect companies to track their expenses and their income, and do so accurately. Yet we tolerate much less from ourselves.

The Need

Last year I got Marco a GPS for Christmas. Around the same time, I upgraded my smartphone to one that has a built-in GPS app. We've become GPS junkies in just a few months. I plug in my destination's address, hit Navigate, and am coached from point A to point B.

Before I had a GPS I used maps. I often printed out maps from online and would even print out step-by-step driving directions. Those tools charted my course. They were powerless, though, to keep me on track once I started. The value of a GPS over a map or even written directions is that the GPS identifies my real-time location and lays it against the course I'm supposed to be taking. If they are misaligned, which they sometimes are (I often get mixed up when I drive), then it reroutes me so I get back on track toward my destination.

Why Track Spending?

Your spending plan and debt snowball plan are a road map and driving directions that take you to a new financial destiny. Expense tracking is your GPS, the tool that keeps you on course while you navigate the route.

Where physical health is concerned, some physicians recommend that patients keep a food log. We've heard that we are what we eat, and food is integrally tied to our body's overall well-being, so that isn't surprising. Dr. Michael Dansinger, a weight-loss and nutrition advisor on *The Biggest Loser*, has gone so far as to *require* every patient to keep a thorough diary of what they eat. He has seen that those who take the task seriously achieve far greater results than those patients who don't. He says, "In my view recording food intake is practically a prerequisite to success."[1]

What Dr. Dansinger has observed related to food logs and improved physical well-being, I've seen with expense tracking and financial health. If you participate in this discipline of tracking your spending, then your chances of long-term financial success are greater than those who refuse. There are a lot of reasons why I believe this is true.

You'll spend less money

The simple fact that you have to account for everything you spend will make you think twice before you make a purchase. Ask me how I know? I keep track of where my money goes, so I have an increased awareness about my spending. That awareness helps me avoid impulses and fosters overall spending restraint. Sometimes it sounds like this in my mind: *Do I really want Marco to see that I've gone out to lunch three times this week? No, I don't think so. I'll skip it.*

Helps you correct problems

Like the GPS that tells you when you get off course, reviewing your actual expenses compared with your spending plan is what keeps you on course. Without checking your progress against your goals, how will you know when problems come up?

For Marco and me, one area of struggle was eating out. We consistently overspent on our eating-out budget. Each month we'd see it when we'd examine our spending and have a conversation about how to curb that habit. Eventually, when it seemed like nothing was working, Marco suggested a radical solution. That's when we started our thirty-day no-eating-out challenge. We went for an entire thirty days without eating out at all. We didn't have one lunch out. No dinner. No coffee on the way to work. Nothing.

In those thirty days we developed new habits that corrected our harmful spending behavior. It's been years since that thirty-day break from restaurants, and we've been able to enjoy dining out in moderation ever since.

Had we not tracked our spending, we wouldn't have realized the extent of our poor habit and wouldn't have been able to correct it.

It's a quick win

Changing your financial situation is first and foremost about attitude and motivation. Second, it is about budget worksheets and number crunching. Tracking your spending is an immediate tangible success for you.

It may take a few months before you pay off the first debt or before you've truly left old attitudes behind, but right now you can pat yourself on the back for doing something right—tracking expenses. It's like putting a checkmark in the "I've done something financially responsible today" column, which feels really, really good. The positive energy you get from doing something smart with your money can sustain you until you achieve a larger goal.

Requires you to regularly pay attention to your financial situation

When your finances feel out of control, it's really hard to want to look at them. And when you don't look at them, they get more out of control. It can become a vicious cycle of overspending leading to avoidance, which creates guilt and leads to more overspending.

When you routinely pay attention to your money, you'll be more apt to take action. It's like the time my car was making an unusual noise every time I braked. I mentioned it to Marco, since he tends to our car repairs, and he didn't seem overly concerned. It bothered me, though, because every time I drove somewhere, I heard this unsettling sound. I mentioned it a couple other times, but Marco still didn't take action.

One day we ended up taking my car somewhere, versus our minivan, which is what he normally drives. Within minutes of heading out he said, "Wow, the brakes sound terrible. When we get home I need to look at them." I'd told him that something was amiss with the brakes, but he wasn't motivated to resolve the problem until he dealt with it himself.

That's what happens when we pay attention to our finances. We see the situation, good and bad, for ourselves, and are compelled to take action.

Creates opportunities for celebration

You have a level of determination to operate within a spending plan and use a debt snowball plan to eliminate debt. On your road to success, you'll do a thousand things right. You'll pay cash for your son's traveling baseball team and successfully reduce your grocery bill by 25 percent. Tracking your expenses lets you see each one of those milestones so you can celebrate it.

I remember how much confidence we gained each time we witnessed ourselves doing something positive with our money. After so many years of feeling financially stagnant, it was exhilarating to see us make better choices. Each of those little successes was like fuel in our tank that kept us moving in our journey.

Facilitates communication

Before we changed our attitudes toward money, Marco and I argued quite a bit about financial matters. Now we rarely argue about money. It isn't that we always agree; we have plenty of disagreements about our financial priorities and our spending. What's changed is the process and information we use to communicate about those disagreements.

Tracking our spending keeps us continually talking about our priorities and goals, which is a tension diffuser for us. We objectively look at our previous month's spending and talk matter-of-factly about it. No more getting angry at one another because our finances feel tight. Instead we say, "The numbers don't lie!"

If one of us overspends, the truth comes out in the numbers. Getting angry doesn't change what has already happened. Instead, we can dissect what happened, learn from it, and work together to make next month better.

How to Track Spending

When you hear *expense tracking*, you might get images of receipts stacked to the ceiling, hours in front of the computer keying everything into a spreadsheet, and then ad nauseam number crunching. For all except the most Type A person among us (I'm raising my hand as one of those Type A folks), you'd rather pluck out your own eyelashes than do that. Blech.

So, sure, you can do what I did in 2006 and start an Excel worksheet that acts like a giant check register. You can create pivot tables, graphs, and charts that slice and dice your spending in every way known to man. But you don't have to do that. You have a range of software options that will do a huge bulk of this work for you. Let me share some of my favorites with you.

Mint.com

Mint.com is the most hands-free solution I know of. You create a free account at Mint.com, then connect that account to all your other financial accounts. Mint.com automatically imports all the transactions that are processed through your linked accounts, whether checking, saving, credit or debit card transactions, then does its best to categorize the expenses for you. For instance, it is smart enough to know that Starbucks is a restaurant and should be classified as "eating out." It likely won't know that the mom-and-pop pizza place around the corner is a restaurant, since Mama D's could be just about any type of business. That's okay, because you can specify Mama D's as a restaurant just once and it'll always categorize it as such moving forward.

You can access a ton of very cool, useful reports that break down your spending. You can integrate components of your own spending plan, like maybe you don't want to spend more than $600 per month on groceries. If you go over that limit, it'll email or text you (or I say you set it up to text your spouse, especially if you are prone to impulse shopping!) so you're aware. They have free mobile apps so you can access your spending information anytime.

Before I move on, let me talk about Mint.com's security. Yes, I said that Mint.com can become a virtually hands-free way to see what and where you spend because it imports your purchasing data from bank accounts and credit cards that you've linked. To use Mint.com, you will give it read-only access to your account information by providing your online banking username and password. This makes some people really nervous, and rightfully so.

Personally, I trust Mint.com for three reasons. First, they use the same 128-bit encryption and physical security that banks use. Second, it is read-only access, so Mint.com does not have permission to initiate any transactions. All they can do is download the data of what has already been done. Third, Mint.com is owned by Intuit, who owns reputable software like TurboTax, QuickBooks, and Quicken.

If you're uncomfortable with this solution, that's fine. There are other options for you.

Quicken

Intuit's Quicken has been around for almost two decades and is a very popular personal financial management software. Where Mint.com is an Internet-based software, Quicken is a PC- or Mac-based software that is installed on a computer.

Although it does not automatically import your transactions like Mint.com, you can import your transaction data in a number of supported file formats. In my experience, most banks offer Quicken-compatible file formats as free downloads from inside the banks' website. Once you get the hang of importing your data, it won't take long to do it each month.

Like Mint.com, you classify expenses into categories, and Quicken will remember those classifications moving forward.

You get access to a variety of reports on your spending, similar to those available on Mint.com.

Quicken provides some basic forward-looking reports that are unavailable in Mint.com. Not every type of expense is included in their cash flow projections, but major bills are. This is a nice visual planning tool. Quicken is not free to use. You pay a one-time license fee and then can use that software as long as it is installed on your computer.

Microsoft Money

In 2009 Microsoft retired its paid-for versions of Money, its personal financial management software. As part of its phaseout, Microsoft has made free sunset versions of Money available for download at Microsoft.com/Downloads; search for "Money Sunset Version."

These free versions provide basic functionality that is similar to what you'll find in Quicken. You can import your bank and credit card transaction information into Money Sunset using Money-compatible files supplied by most banks (these are the same file types Quicken supports).

Before you start using Money, be aware that the only technical support available for this software is online. That makes this software a good fit for those who are slightly more tech-savvy.

You Need a Budget

Although I'm not normally a fan of the word *budget*, I like this software called You Need a Budget. It is available in an online version or as a CD-ROM that can be downloaded to your computer. Like Quicken, you pay a one-time fee for a one-user license.

You Need a Budget is distinct from the other financial tools mentioned because of its planning components. You can track your spending and import files from your bank like you do with Quicken or Money, but you can also do a whole lot more.

Beyond historical tracking, You Need a Budget wants you to break free from paycheck-to-paycheck living. Yes, you give every dollar a job, based on what you established in your spending plan, and you set up savings goals for those non-routine expenses that typically bust your budget, but after that, you focus on building savings so you have a buffer against future needs.

I personally use You Need a Budget and love it. It gives me the historical data I can get from Mint.com or Quicken, but makes saving much easier for the goals we discussed in chapter 4.

But I Buy Everything on Credit Cards

Many people have told me over the years that they don't need to track expenses because they pay for everything, and I mean e-v-e-r-y-t-h-i-n-g, with their credit card. They pay their credit card off each month and rely on the reports from their credit card company that break down their spending.

I'm not a fan of this approach and wouldn't recommend it to anyone ever. It is a proven fact that consumers spend more when they purchase using plastic rather than cash.[2] Buying something on plastic distances us from the pain of paying and helps us feel good about our purchase, whereas paying with cash is painful, since we hate to part with our money.[3] You can tell me that you are the exception to this rule, but I still disagree. You spend more when you pay with plastic because your money is not as real to you, plus you don't have the same boundaries that cash creates.

Also, more often than not, you can't keep up paying the balance in full each month. I fell back into credit card debt on two separate occasions as I told myself that I would only charge what I could pay for at month's end. At some point I didn't want to or couldn't pay the entire balance and started on a slippery slope into debt.

If some of you are saying, "Yeah, but I get all these rewards from my credit card. I use it exclusively because I'm a very savvy consumer and am, in essence, getting something for nothing," here is one final thought: Friends, credit cards offer rewards because you spend more when they are there.[4] Proceed with caution, because this is dangerous ground.

There are enough automated expense tracking solutions available that I don't think you need a credit card to do that job for you.

Using the Information You've Got

Tracking expenses isn't a magic formula that, when you do it, *poof!* your finances turn around overnight. The transformational power of expense tracking comes when you use the information as a decision-making guide. There is no power in mindless behavior. Measure your progress against your goals. Let your past expenses help you see where you need correction. Talk with those who share your finances about trends and patterns so that you can plan for a better future.

13

helpful hints
for reducing expenses

*Y*ou've done all you can to balance your spending plan, but your combined savings and expenses still outpace your income. Before you start slashing the amounts you set aside into your emergency fund and toward your goals, I'd encourage you to consider reducing your household expenses wherever possible.

I have a website dedicated to sharing money-saving ideas, coupon strategies, and real-time deals and legitimate freebies at PocketYourDollars.com. The site would be a great resource for you as you work to spend less money for a life you still enjoy living. Its focus is more time-limited savings opportunities versus timeless savings strategies.

Therefore, I'm taking this chapter to share with you ways to increase your monthly cash flow without having to get a second job.

Tax Withholdings

Millions of Americans get an annual tax refund from the IRS. These refunds aren't a gift or free money from the IRS. It is called a refund because it is *your* money that you have overpaid and are getting back. Considering that the average tax refund was $2,913 in 2011, that's a $242 per month overpayment.[1]

I'd encourage you to consider modifying the amount of tax you withhold from your paycheck. Marco and I had always had the maximum amount withheld from our paychecks so that we'd receive the largest refund possible. We used a variety of online calculators, like those found at Bankrate.com (www.bankrate.com/calculators/index-of-taxes-calculators .aspx), and adjusted our withholdings when we started to get out of debt.

We didn't want to owe money to the IRS at tax time, but we didn't want to get a hefty refund either. Instead, we aimed to pay just a little more than what we thought we'd owe. Our refund dropped from thousands of dollars to just a few hundred, but that meant we put hundreds of dollars back into our monthly budget.

Since we had been saving money, we weren't afraid of the off chance that we'd owe a little to the IRS. We'd done our due diligence to investigate what our proper withholdings should be, so if it turned out we had underpaid our taxes, we didn't expect it to be by much. We knew we'd have the money in savings to cover it.

Cable Television

There are ways that you can watch a lot of the cable content you enjoy without having to pay eighty to a hundred dollars per month for it. Thanks to the Internet you can view, or stream, a lot of content online that used to be exclusively available on the tube.

There are websites, some free and some you have to pay for, that provide thousands of hours of programming from new and classic television shows to movies of every genre. Here are a few of the more popular services:

- **iTunes.** iTunes primarily offers pay-per-view content including television shows and movies.
- **Netflix.** Netflix is a paid service that offers a month-to-month contract. It costs less than ten dollars per month, and you are able to stream an unlimited amount of content from Netflix's site—and they have a ton of shows and movies. There are some new-release motion pictures, but none of the television shows are current season. The shows and movies can be viewed on a computer, a tablet device, a smartphone, or a television that is connected to the Internet.
- **Amazon.** Amazon offers a large library of television and movie offers similar to Netflix. As of this writing, its library is not as robust as Netflix, but it is growing almost daily. Their content can be accessed two ways. You can pay-per-view or buy an annual Amazon Prime membership to gain unlimited access for a year. The Amazon Prime membership includes other benefits related to Amazon.com as well, and is an overall better value than Netflix.
- **Hulu.** Hulu is a free-to-use website that catalogs up to the five most recent episodes of current-season television shows and recent movies from numerous big-name production houses. Hulu.com can only be viewed on

a computer or a TV connected to a computer via an HDMI cable.

- **Hulu Plus.** Hulu Plus is a membership-based extension of Hulu. For a fee of less than ten dollars per month you can watch all the current-season episodes of popular shows from a number of major networks. As of this writing, it is the only legal service I know of that offers current season content. Content from Hulu Plus is able to be streamed on computers, Internet-connected TVs, gaming consoles, smartphones, and more.

There are three primary ways you can hook your TV into the Internet:

1. **Use a gaming console.** Devices like an Xbox, Wii, or Kinect gaming console can be used to connect your television to the Internet.
2. **Buy a special device.** Roku and Apple both make devices specially designed to connect your TV to the Internet and give you access to programming channels. You buy the device one time and gain access to certain free programming; you can pay a small monthly fee to access additional programming.
3. **Use a laptop or other computer.** With an HDMI cable connected between a computer and your television, your TV screen becomes a giant computer monitor. Whatever you view on your computer screen will appear on your TV screen.

If you are loyal to cable and want to keep it, or some form of paid television programming, then I'd encourage you to spend a few minutes at BillShrink.com. You enter in your must-have channels and zip code, then are presented with a side-by-side comparison of the various television subscription options available to you. It will help ensure you aren't overpaying.

Gasoline

The quickest and easiest way to save money at the gas pump is to buy your gasoline on Tuesdays. Think about it: On Thursday nights and Fridays people fill up in anticipation of the weekend. Then over the weekend and on Mondays, folks buy gas to get ready for the week. Tuesday and Wednesday tend to be the slowest days for gas sales, and as a result, prices dip.

Also, find the lowest gas prices near you using GasBuddy.com. GasBuddy also has a mobile app with GPS capability to direct you to the cheapest station near you nationwide.

Eating Out

If Marco and I have to name a downfall in our personal financial management, it is eating out. Now we're a family of four, and although our girls are still young, we spend half as much on restaurants as we did five and six years ago, when we were two single adults. That's due, in part, to our figuring out where and how to get coupons so we can avoid full-priced meals.

- **Restaurant.com.** At the Restaurant.com website, you can buy gift certificates for thousands of different restaurants nationwide. Typically, their $25 certificates sell for $10, but every month Restaurant.com runs promotions. During an 80-percent-off promotion, you can buy that $25 certificate for 80 percent off, or just $2. The gift certificate does not expire, so there's no harm buying a few in advance on sale. There is a caveat with the gift certificates from Restaurant.com, though. Each one requires some sort of minimum in-restaurant purchase. For instance, a $25 gift certificate might require you to buy $35 worth of appetizers, entrées, drinks, and desserts *before* the $25 certificate can be applied. That means your total expense for a $35 meal would look something like this:

$35 bill for food and drinks

  − $25 gift certificate from Restaurant.com

  + $2 cost for buying coupon on sale at Restaurant .com

  = $12 (before tip)

$12 + tip = total cost of $35 meal

- **Valpak.** Almost every household in America gets blue envelopes full of local coupons from Valpak. Yes, they are a fine resource for dining coupons, but I actually prefer Valpak's mobile app. When we decide to eat out while running errands, I check the Valpak app on my phone to see if there are any current offers near us.
- **Daily deal sites.** Sites like Groupon and Living Social often sell discounts for local restaurants. With these offers you pay something in advance, say $10, and that gets you $20 worth of food or drink at the establishment. You have a limited time within which you can redeem your $20 credit. After that time frame you lose the promotional or "extra" value you bought, but you can still redeem your coupon for the amount you paid out of pocket. To find daily deals for your area, I recommend Yipit.com as a single website that aggregates daily deals by city from hundreds of one-deal-per-day websites.

Mobile Phones

Have you ever gotten a free phone when you sign a two-year contract with a mobile carrier? Me too. Don't do that again, okay? Your "free" phone, friend, is not free. Mobile carriers have two types of plans—those for people on contract and those for people who do not have a contract (also called prepaid plans). For the same plan—quantity of minutes, texts, and data usage—contract fees are different. That's how they can afford to give you a "free" phone. You pay for it in a more expensive monthly plan.

A better option is to save your money so you can buy a phone outright at the time you need one. I've found that I don't need a new phone every two years anyway, since I purpose to take good care of my things.

Once you're free from your current contract, you have a handful of options. Most major carriers offer some variety of prepaid plans. In my experience, that information is not always easy to find on their websites, so you may need to call their customer service number or visit a store to get details on what they offer. But major carriers aren't your only option. Two smaller mobile networks have the best prices I've been able to find:

- **Boost Mobile.** With Boost Mobile (www.boostmobile.com), you choose from a limited selection of phones, but your monthly fee for unlimited talk and text is $45. For each six-month period that you pay your bill on time, your monthly fee drops by $5 until you pay a minimum of $30 per month.
- **Straight Talk.** If unlimited talk and text isn't enough and you want mobile web access too, then Straight Talk (www.straighttalk.com) is a great option—you can get

all that for $45 per month. The upside: Their network supports many different phones, including iPhones, after you buy a Straight Talk SIM card for less than $20. The catch: Their web access is fairly limited—no streaming radio, Netflix, or data-intensive games—but basic functions like email, popular social media sites, weather, and theater times are included.

Groceries

Contrary to popular belief, coupons are *not* the primary way to reduce your grocery bill. Being price-smart is the primary strategy.

First, be sure you understand what a good regular price is for a core set of groceries you routinely buy. I'd recommend that you write out a list of ten to fifteen items, then do a price comparison at a number of local stores. Your goal is to identify which store has the best prices on most of the things you routinely buy. Then you can switch to using that store for a bulk of your purchases and save as much as 10 percent without ever clipping a coupon.

A few years back when I did this price comparison, I found that the store where I had been shopping was five to fifteen cents more expensive on every single item I purchased than a competitor that was equidistant from my house. Not all grocery retailers are created equal.

Places we call "grocery stores" tend to have higher everyday prices than "hard discounters" like Aldi and dollar stores or big-box retailers like Target and Walmart. If you've been a lifelong grocery store shopper, I'd encourage you to price compare at some other venues and see how much you'd save.

I'm often asked here if I think warehouse clubs, where you pay an annual membership fee, are worth the money. My answer always is "It depends." You can add a warehouse club into your price comparison and see for yourself. Yes, a warehouse club will often beat the everyday prices at a grocery store, but I've found their prices, for the things I buy, to be neck-and-neck with stores like Aldi and Walmart. I can't find enough discounted products at warehouse clubs to make it worth the annual fee.

That's also true because I am willing to shop the sales. I think you can shave 30 to 40 percent—if not more—off your grocery bill if you are able to buy what you need when it is on sale versus waiting until you need it. For instance, my family uses barbecue sauce in a number of different recipes; over the course of a year I may use three or four bottles. The cheapest regular price for the brand of sauce we prefer is about $2.75. However, a few times each year the sauce we like goes on sale for 88 cents per bottle. I pick up three or four bottles and save almost $2 each. On an individual product, $2 may not seem significant, but consider how a few dollars for *each item you buy all year* would add up.

I encourage you to take that same list of ten to fifteen core grocery items you routinely buy, and pay attention to their sale prices and how frequently they go on sale. I had always thought an item had two prices: its regular price and its sale price. I figured that if I saw something on sale, then it was at its "sale price" and I should buy it. I was wrong.

Every item has multiple price points including its regular price and numerous sale prices. As a consumer, you need to figure out what the lowest sale price is for the things you buy and how often the item goes on sale at that price. When you know those two things, you can buy enough quantity on sale to get you through to the next sale.

There are two helpful considerations as you do this. First, groceries, even nonperishable items and personal care items, have a seasonal nature to their sales cycles. When you buy groceries in season, just like buying produce in season, you get a better price. Second, most in-season items are on sale at least once every six to eight weeks, if not more.

Time of the year	Products
New Year's	• Healthy foods and weight-loss products: salad dressing, croutons, protein bars, diet shakes
Week before the Super Bowl	• Things for grilling and Super Bowl parties: bratwurst, chicken wings, condiments, chips, pizza, charcoal briquettes
Valentine's Day	• Beginning of springtime product sales
Lent	• Fish, fishsticks, boxed macaroni and cheese
Spring	• Things for picnics and allergies: paper plates, bug spray, swimmer's diapers, allergy medicine, lemonade drink mix
Easter	• End of wintertime product sales
Week before Cinco de Mayo	• Tex-Mex foods: taco shells, ground beef, avocados
Summer	• Continuation of springtime products • Items for grilling and outdoor activities: hamburger and hot dog buns, baked beans, charcoal briquettes, bandages, and antibiotic ointment
August 1	• Beginning of fall product sales • Lunch box foods: peanut butter, jelly, fruit snacks, juice boxes • Hot foods and foods that require baking: frozen lasagna, canned soup, frozen vegetables • Fall cleaning products
Labor Day	• Beginning of sales for baking supplies and Halloween candy • Best prices on candy typically this month
Winter	• Continuation of fall product sales • Winter items: hot beverages like tea and cocoa, cough and cold medicine, facial tissues, oatmeal and hot cereal

I believe you can save as much or more by buying products on sale as you would if you paid full price with a coupon. Let me illustrate with a example.

In this weekend's paper there was a coupon for $1 off a box of crackers. You add crackers to your shopping list for the week and pay $2.50 at the register—the full price of $3.50 less the $1-off coupon. If you wait a few weeks, you'll see that crackers routinely go on sale for $2 per box. That means the sale price without a coupon is *less than* what you paid for crackers having used a coupon.

It's only once you understand what a good regular and sale price is that it makes sense to introduce grocery coupons. If you think about our cracker example, what if you waited until they were on sale for $2 per box and *then* used your $1-off coupon. You'd get a $3.50 box of crackers for a buck. That's a steal, friends. The primary savings comes from the sale, and the secondary source of savings from the coupon.

Coupon Filing System

The days of having to clip every coupon from the Sunday paper and manage a file box with thousands of coupons that all expire a few weeks from now are done. The Internet gives us the ability to use online databases to locate coupons when we need them.

I use a clip-free grocery coupon system. Every Sunday I get the paper and take the coupon magazine insert thingys, as I affectionately call them (for the record their formal name is "free-standing inserts," or FSIs), and write the date of the Sunday paper from which I got them on the cover. I also take note of the publisher that printed the insert. The publisher's name is printed across the top and is typically Smart Source, Red Plum, P&G, or General Mills.

Then I set the whole entire insert, *no coupons clipped out of it*, in a file folder with the newest ones in the back. This keeps my inserts in chronological order so I can easily find what I need if I know the date and publisher for any coupon. For instance, if an online coupon database tells me that a coupon was in the March 22 Smart Source insert, then I can easily locate that coupon from within its insert.

My website, PocketYourDollars.com, has one of these free coupon databases that you can use to locate coupons for items you want to buy. The database includes coupons from the newspaper, but also legitimate coupons that can be printed from the Internet and coupons found within various magazines.

I make this whole thing even easier for you by compiling shopping lists—sale items with their corresponding coupons—for several national retailers each week. All the shopping lists are free to use and can be found at PocketYour Dollars.com.

Online Shopping

I buy almost everything online, from shoes to toys to our most recent garbage disposal. There are three things I'd recommend for saving money when you shop online:

Shop through a cash-back site

Sites like PocketYourDollarsRewards.com and Ebates.com offer an automatic cash rebate for nearly all online purchases when you start from that portal. You can earn anywhere from 1 to 15 percent of your spending back in cash when you shop through one of these sites.

Here's how it works:

• You create a free account with one of these cash-back sites.
• You initiate all your online shopping at your cash-back site. For instance, you go to PocketYourDollarsRewards .com and log in, then search the site to find Macys.com, or whichever online retailer you need to visit.
• You click on the appropriate link to enter the retailer's website, and make your online purchase as usual.
• A percentage of what you spend at the online retailer will be deposited as cash into your PocketYourDollars Rewards or Ebates account. You don't need to fill out any paperwork. It's automatic but not immediate; it can take a few weeks for your deposit to appear in your account.
• You are mailed a check each quarter for your earnings.

Sites like this operate on a legitimate business model where they are paid a commission for all the online sales originated at their site. They share a portion of that commission with you. There are dozens and dozens of these sites available, but many are not reputable. I'd encourage you to stick with the ones I recommend, or thoroughly research any site before you join.

Use a coupon

Most online shoppers are savvy to look for coupon codes and promotional discounts for every purchase they make. Sites like PocketYourDollarsRewards and Ebates will show you any available coupon codes for the retailer you are pursuing. You can use those authorized codes and still earn cash back.

My website, PocketYourDollars.com, also offers a free database of coupon codes for hundreds of online retailers.

These coupons offer everything from free shipping to money off your purchase.

Live Well for Less

It's fitting that we end this book, *Pocket Your Dollars*, by helping you learn how to pocket your dollars. You can enjoy life while spending less money to do it. However, frugal living habits alone aren't enough to change your financial destiny. Their power magnifies when they're combined with grateful, satisfied, future-looking, generous attitudes.

acknowledgments

*T*he message for this book came to me in the fall of 2009. I had been invited to teach a class for employees at General Mills about how to get out and stay out of debt. It was the first time I stood to teach on the topic, outside of my friends and family. The core of my message was captured in a single PowerPoint slide, titled "Five Attitudes That Keep You Broke."

As I taught that class, and many others since then, the message about financial attitudes has resonated. People always laugh when I open the class by saying "I did not bring a budget worksheet with me today. Lack of a budget worksheet is not what has caused your financial problems. Your attitudes have caused your problems."

Meeting Donna

Fast-forward a few years. I got an email from someone named Donna who said she'd seen me mention in a blog post that I'd love to write a book one day. She said she worked for a book publisher and asked if I'd consider writing one for them.

I didn't think she was serious. See, I get a lot of crazy emails and thought hers might be one. Plus, if she really did work for a book publisher, what's to say she even has influence about which authors they bring on board?

My response was a polite, "Who exactly are you and what exactly do you do?"

Her response was something like, "I am Donna Carpenter. I work in talent acquisition for Bethany House and was recently tasked to recruit more nonfiction female authors. You'd be my first recruit. Are you interested in going to coffee?"

Whoa. It was legit. I called Marco over to the computer and let him read the email thread. Within days, Marco and I met Donna and her colleague, Andy McGuire, for coffee.

I told them about the "Five Attitudes That Keep You Broke" PowerPoint slide. They loved the idea. I knew it would resonate with people. The stage was set for this book.

Writing

It took fifteen months for me to complete the rough draft. I did not do it alone.

My husband, Marco, supported me all the way. He took our two young girls to a cabin up north for a week, by himself, to give me space to write. He cooked, cleaned, bathed, soothed, and cared for our children for weeks—turned into months—so that I could complete this work. He also allowed me to share our lives in ways that felt sometimes too real and too personal. Thank you, Marco, for letting our tests become testimonies. I love you.

My two precious girls, Victoria Joy and Olivia Grace, gave up their mommy for months so that you'd have this book to read. Thank you, girls, for being living examples of generosity.

Laura Wales, my right hand at PocketYourDollars.com, worked double and triple time in my stead to lead and guide my website and its community while I wrote. She encouraged me every step of the way (and her husband, Eli, encouraged her). Without her, my ship would have sunk more than once. Thank you.

Renee, Amber, the rest of the PocketYourDollars.com team, and the entire PocketYourDollars.com community supported me. They picked up the slack, prayed for me, and did amazing work while I was focused on this project. Thank you.

My dad and stepmom, as well as my dear friends Angie and Tim Erickson, allowed me to use their homes as quiet writing retreats. I could never have made my deadline without you. Thank you.

Donna, Andy, and the entire team at Bethany House have been amazing to work with. Thank you for teaching me how to write a book. Thank you for allowing me to share these attitudes far and wide.

I pray your life will be transformed as you see how your attitudes have influenced your behavior and you learn how to change that pattern.

I'd love to hear from you at carrie@pocketyourdollars.com with stories of how this book has impacted you and your family.

notes

Chapter 1: My Story

1. *Wikipedia*, s.v. "Economic history of Brazil," last modified June 4, 2012, http://en.wikipedia.org/wiki/Economic_history_of_Brazil.

2. *Dictionary.com*, s.v. "attitude," accessed September 14, 2012, http://dictionary.reference.com/browse/attitude.

3. Susan J. Currya, Louis Grothausa, and Colleen McBridea, "Reasons for Quitting: Intrinsic and Extrinsic Motivation for Smoking Cessation in a Population-Based Sample of Smokers" (Center for Health Studies, Group Health Cooperative of Puget Sound USA, June 1998).

4. Ibid.

Chapter 2: If Only I Had More Money

1. Hope Gurion, "Living Paycheck to Paycheck," CNN/CareerBuilder.com, October 8, 2008, http://www.cnn.com/2008/LIVING/worklife/10/08/cb.workers.paycheck/index.html.

2. Robert Snell, "How Talented Ex-Ute, Ex-Lion Luther Elliss Went Bankrupt," *Standard-Examiner*, January 20, 2010, http://www.standard.net/topics/sports/2010/01/19/how-talented-ex-ute-ex-lion-luther-elliss-went-bankrupt.

3. Jack Hough, "Why Lottery Winners Go Bankrupt," *SmartMoney*, March 28, 2011, http://www.smartmoney.com/invest/stocks/why-lottery-winners-go-bankrupt-1301002181742/.

4. Neil T. Anderson, *The Bondage Breaker* (Eugene, Oregon: Harvest House, 1993), 194–196.

5. Ibid., 197.

Chapter 3: I Deserve a Treat

1. Denise K. Schull, "Feelings Matter—Even in Investing Decisions," *Market Mind Games* (blog), *Psychology Today*, March 12, 2012, http://www.psychologytoday.com/blog/market-mind-games/201203/feelings-matter-even-in-investing-decisions.

2. Tara Parker-Pope, "This Is Your Brain at the Mall: Why Shopping Makes You Feel So Good," Health Journal, *Wall Street Journal*, December 6, 2005, http://online.wsj.com/ad/article/cigna/SB113382650575214543.html.

3. Ibid.

4. Ibid.

5. Ibid.

Chapter 4: It Won't Happen to Me

1. *Wikipedia*, s.v. "2004 Hendrick Motorsports aircraft crash," last modified August 13, 2012, http://en.wikipedia.org/wiki/2004_Hendrick_Motorsports_aircraft_crash.

2. Ibid.

Chapter 5: I'll Fake It 'Til I Make It

1. Hillary Mayell, "As Consumerism Spreads, Earth Suffers, Study Says," *National Geographic News*, January 12, 2004, http://news.nationalgeographic.com/news/2004/01/0111_040112_consumerism.html.

2. Sheyna Steiner, "5 Economic Indicators to Watch," *Bankrate.com*, accessed September 14, 2012, http://www.bankrate.com/finance/investing/5-economic-indicators-to-watch-1.aspx.

3. Candace Webb, "How to Change Consumer Behavior Through Advertising," *Houston Chronicle*, accessed September 14, 2012, http://smallbusiness.chron.com/change-consumer-behavior-through-advertising-11281.html.

4. Richard McKenzie and Dwight Lee, *Microeconomics for MBAs: The Economic Way of Thinking for Managers* (New York: Cambridge University Press, 2010), chapter 4.

5. Michael Solomon, "Who Got the Better Ring?", *Elle*, April 19, 2012, http://www.elle.com/pop-culture/best/who-got-the-better-ring-654804#slide-6.

6. Alexander Spradlin, "Fake It 'Til You Make It," *The Empathetic Misanthrope* (blog), *Psychology Today*, September 11, 2011, http://www.psychologytoday.com/blog/the-empathic-misanthrope/201109/fake-it-til-you-make-it.

7. Thomas J. Stanley, *The Millionaire Mind* (Kansas City, MO: Andrews McMeel, 2000), 4.

8. Thomas Stanley and William Danko, *The Millionaire Next Door: The Surprising Secrets of America's Wealthy* (Atlanta: Longstreet Press, 1996), 9. Number was adjusted for inflation from the $131,000 quoted in the book using the Inflation Calculator at www.westegg.com/inflation. All subsequent adjustments were made using the same Inflation Calculator.

9. Stanley, *The Millionaire Mind*, 9.

10. Ibid. The 1996 number was $1.6 million in net worth; adjusted for inflation.

11. Stanley and Danko, *The Millionaire Next Door*, 13.

12. Stanley, *The Millionaire Mind*, 73.

13. Stanley and Danko, *The Millionaire Next Door*, 11.

14. Stanley, *The Millionaire Mind*, 26.

15. Ibid.

16. Stanley and Danko, *The Millionaire Next Door*, 31. Figure is adjusted for inflation from the 1996 number listed in the book.

17. Stanley, *The Millionaire Mind*, 26.

18. Stanley and Danko, *The Millionaire Next Door*, 112–113.

19. Ibid.

20. Ibid.

21. Ibid., 9. Number adjusted for inflation from the $320,000 number cited in the book.

22. Ibid., 35. Number adjusted for inflation.

23. Ibid., 9.

24. Renee Riva, *Guido's Gondola*, illus. Steve Bjorkman (Colorado Springs: WaterBrook, 2005).

Chapter 6: I Can't Afford It

1. "Homeless Man Leaves Behind Surprise: $4 Million," NPR's *All Things Considered*, July 27, 2009, http://www.npr.org/2009/07/27/111091624/homeless-man-leaves-behind-surprise-4-million and *Wikipedia*, s.v. "Richard Leroy Walters," last modified December 21, 2010, http://en.wikipedia.org/wiki/Richard_Leroy_Walters.

2. *Online Etymology Dictionary*, s.v. "miserable," accessed September 14, 2012, http://www.etymonline.com/index.php?term=miserable.

3. *Dictionary.com*, s.v. "greed," accessed September 14, 2012, http://dictionary.reference.com/browse/greed.

4. James Hall, review of *Michelangelo: A Tormented Life* by Antonio Forcellino, *Observer*, October 10, 2009, http://www.guardian.co.uk/books/2009/oct/11/michelangelo-tormented-life-forcellino.

5. *Wikipedia*, s.v. "Michelangelo," last modified July 14, 2012, http://en.wikipedia.org/wiki/Michelangelo.

6. Devin Tooma, "Crazy Dead Men," *The Florentine*, March 24, 2011, http://www.theflorentine.net/articles/article-view.asp?issuetocId=6700.

7. Bruce Johnston, "Michelangelo Is Branded a 'Multi-millionaire' Miser," *Telegraph*, November 30, 2002, http://www.telegraph.co.uk/news/worldnews/europe/italy/1414836/Michelangelo-is-branded-a-multi-millionaire-miser.html.

8. P. H. Silverstone, "Is Chronic Low Self-Esteem the Cause of Eating Disorders?", *Medical Hypotheses* 39 (1992), 311–315.

9. Jessie Sholl, "What Is the Difference Between Compulsive Hoarding and Collecting?", *Dirty Secret* (blog), *Psychology Today*, December 17, 2010, http://www.psychologytoday.com/blog/dirty-secret/201012/what-is-the-difference-between-compulsive-hoarding-and-collecting.

10. "Life During the Great Depression," AllAboutHistory.org, accessed September 14, 2012, http://www.allabouthistory.org/life-during-the-great-depression.htm.

11. Ibid.

12. Elizabeth W. Dunn, Claire E. Ashton-James, Margaret D. Hanson, and Lara B. Akin, "On the Costs of Self-interested Economic Behavior: How Does

Stinginess Get Under the Skin?", *Journal of Health Psychology* 15 (2010): 627–633, http://laraaknin.psych.ubc.ca/files/2011/09/Dunn-Ashton-James-Hanson-Aknin-2010.pdf.

13. Lara B. Aknin and Elizabeth W. Dunn, "Spending Money on Others Promotes Happiness," *Science* 319 (2008): 1687–1688.

Chapter 7: Changing Your Self-Talk

1. Association for Psychological Science, "Thoughts That Win," press release, March 25, 2011, http://www.psychologicalscience.org/index.php/news/releases/thoughts-that-win.html.

2. "Positive Thinking: Reduce Stress by Eliminating Negative Self-Talk," Mayo Clinic, May 28, 2011, http://www.mayoclinic.com/health/positive-thinking/SR00009.

3. *Wikipedia*, s.v. "Cognitive behavioral therapy," last modified September 11, 2012, http://en.wikipedia.org/wiki/Cognitive_behavioral_therapy.

Chapter 8: Standing Up to Pressure

1. Kirsten Weir, "The Power of Self-Control," *Monitor on Psychology 43*, no. 1 (January 2012): 36, http://www.apa.org/monitor/2012/01/self-control.aspx.

2. *Wikipedia*, s.v. "David Blaine," last modified September 12, 2012, http://en.wikipedia.org/wiki/David_blaine.

3. Deborah Kotz, "How Willpower Works," *Boston Globe*, November 7, 2011, http://www.bostonglobe.com/lifestyle/health-wellness/2011/11/07/how-willpower-works/XlOvEG4FipvZ8vM8VUNBpK/story.html.

4. *Wikipedia*, s.v. "David Blaine."

5. Lexi Petronis, "How to Increase Your Willpower," *Woman's Day*, May 18, 2012, http://shine.yahoo.com/healthy-living/increase-willpower-161400177.html.

6. Jane E. Brody, "A Richer Life by Seeing the Glass Half Full," *Well* (blog), *New York Times*, May 21, 2012, http://well.blogs.nytimes.com/2012/05/21/a-richer-life-by-seeing-the-glass-half-full/.

7. Tara Parker-Pope, "How to Boost Your Willpower," *Well* (blog), *New York Times*, December 6, 2007, http://well.blogs.nytimes.com/2007/12/06/how-to-boost-your-willpower/.

8. Ibid.

9. Kelly McGonigal, "The Science of Willpower," *IDEA Fitness Journal 5*, no. 6 (June 2008), http://www.ideafit.com/fitness-library/science-willpower-0.

10. Ibid.

11. M. C. Fiore, C. R. Jaén, T. B. Baker, et al., "Treating Tobacco Use and Dependence: 2008 Update," *Quick Reference Guide for Clinicians* (Rockville, MD: U.S. Department of Health and Human Services), April 2009.

12. E. V. Gifford, B. S. Kohlenberg, S. C. Hayes, D. O. Antonuccio, M. M. Piasecki, M. L. Rasmussen-Hall, et al., "Acceptance-Based Treatment for Smoking Cessation," *Behavior Therapy* 35 (2004), 689–705.

13. "Monthly Averages for Minneapolis, MN," Weather.com, accessed September 14, 2012, http://www.weather.com/weather/wxclimatology/monthly/graph/USMN0503.

14. Adapted from an example found at "Better Distress Tolerance Through ACCEPTS," Dialectical Behavior Therapy of Southern California, April 12, 2011, http://dbttherapy.com/dbt-treatment-distress-tolerance.html.

Chapter 9: Staying in It for the Long Haul

1. Adapted from the four items identified as components in academic resilience as stated in A. J. Martin and H. W. Marsh, "Academic Resilience and the Four Cs: Confidence, Control, Composure, and Commitment" (paper presented at NZARE AARE Conference, Auckland, New Zealand, November 2003).

2. Debra Ollivier, "Rick Newman on 'Rebounders': Turning Setbacks Into Success," The Blog, Huffington Post, May 10, 2012, http://www.huffingtonpost.com/debra-ollivier/rick-newman-rebounders-turning-setbacks-into-success_b_1504044.html.

3. "Thomas A. Edison Quotes," accessed September 14, 2012, http://www.brainyquote.com/quotes/quotes/t/thomasaed132683.html.

4. Wikipedia, s.v. "Thomas Edison," last modified September 13, 2012, http://en.wikipedia.org/wiki/Thomas_Edison.

5. Peter Cohan, "Learning From Brilliant Mistakes," Forbes, December 29, 2011, http://www.forbes.com/sites/petercohan/2011/12/29/learning-from-brilliant-mistakes/.

6. Adapted from Paul J. H. Schoemaker, "Paul J. H. Schoemaker's 'Brilliant Mistakes': Finding Opportunity in Failures," Knowledge @ Wharton, November 9, 2011, http://knowledge.wharton.upenn.edu/article.cfm?articleid=2869.

7. Jim Collins, Good to Great: Why Some Companies Make the Leap . . . and Others Don't (New York: HarperBusiness, 2001), 33–35.

8. Adapted from the steps of self-compassion found at www.self-compassion.org.

9. Ollivier, "Rick Newman on 'Rebounders.'"

10. Alana Horowitz and Vivian Giang, "17 People Who Got Fired Before They Became Rich and Famous," MSN Money Canada, http://money.ca.msn.com/savings-debt/gallery/17-people-who-got-fired-before-they-became-rich-and-famous#image=1, slide 7.

11. Ibid., slide 11.

12. Ibid., slide 2.

13. Wikipedia, s.v. "Fred Astaire," last modified September 17, 2012, http://en.wikipedia.org/wiki/Fred_Astaire.

14. Wikipedia, s.v. "The Beatles' Decca audition," last modified May 7, 2012, http://en.wikipedia.org/wiki/The_Beatles%27_Decca_audition.

Chapter 11: Paying Off Debt

1. Moty Amar, Dan Ariely, Shahar Ayal, Cynthia Cryder, and Scott Rick, "Winning the Battle but Losing the War: The Psychology of Debt Management," Journal of Marketing Research, special issue (2011).

2. Drazen Prelec and Duncan Simester, "Always Leave Home Without It: A Further Investigation of the Credit-Card Effect on Willingness-to-Pay," *Marketing Letters 12*, no. 1 (2001), 11.

3. "About 30 Factors Influence Your Credit Score," Yahoo! Finance, accessed September 17, 2012, http://finance.yahoo.com/education/loan/credit_basics/article/101287/about_30_factors_influence_your_credit_score.

4. Maxine Sweet, "Credit Advice: The Effect on Credit Scores of Paying Off and Closing Credit Cards," Experian, August 5, 2009, http://www.experian.com/ask-experian/20090805-the-effect-on-credit-scores-of-paying-off-and-closing-credit-cards.html.

Chapter 12: Holding Yourself Accountable

1. Michael Dansinger, "Why Should I Keep a Food Record?", *Conquering Diabetes* (blog), WebMD, March 26, 2012, http://blogs.webmd.com/life-with-diabetes-2/2012/03/why-should-i-keep-a-food-record.html.

2. Prelec and Simester, "Always Leave Home Without It," 11.

3. "Get Ready for the 'Pain of Paying,'" *The Daily Beast* (blog), *Newsweek*, August 29, 2008, http://www.thedailybeast.com/newsweek/2008/08/30/get-ready-for-the-pain-of-paying.html.

4. Sumit Agarwal, Sujit Chakravorti, and Anna Lunn, "Why Do Banks Reward Their Customers to Use Their Credit Cards?" (paper, Federal Reserve Bank of Chicago, December 20, 2010), 13.

Chapter 13: Helpful Hints for Reducing Expenses

1. "Filing Season Statistics," IRS, last modified August 4, 2012, http://www.irs.gov/uac/Filing-Season-Statistics----Dec.-31,-2011.

Carrie Rocha (ha-sha) owns and operates PocketYourDollars .com, one of the most popular couponing and personal finance sites on the web. Carrie writes regularly for Bankrate .com and has been featured on *Wall Street Journal Radio, Glamour,* Yahoo! Finance, CNNMoney.com, FoxBusiness .com, and many other magazines and websites. Carrie lives with her husband and two daughters in suburban Minneapolis, Minnesota. Learn more at www.pocketyourdollars.com.

Photo courtesy of Studio D Photo